Colloquial
Spanish

The Colloquial Series

Series adviser: Gary King

The following languages are available in the Colloquial series:

*Afrikaans
*Albanian
*Amharic
Arabic (Levantine)
*Arabic of Egypt
Arabic of the Gulf
and Saudi Arabia
Basque
*Breton
Bulgarian
*Cambodian
*Cantonese
*Chinese
*Croatian and Serbian
*Czech
*Danish
*Dutch
*Estonian
*Finnish
*French
*German
*Greek
Gujarati
*Hebrew
*Hindi
*Hungarian
*Icelandic
*Indonesian
Italian

*Japanese
*Korean
*Latvian
*Lithuanian
Malay
*Mongolian
*Norwegian
Panjabi
*Persian
*Polish
*Portuguese
*Portuguese of Brazil
*Romanian
*Russian
*Scottish Gaelic
*Slovak
*Slovene
Somali
*Spanish
*Spanish of Latin America
*Swahili
*Swedish
*Tamil
*Thai
*Turkish
*Ukranian
Urdu
*Vietnemese
*Welsh

Accompanying cassette(s) (*and CDs) are available for all the above titles. They can be ordered through your bookseller, or send payment with order to Routledge Ltd, ITPS, Cheriton House, North Way, Andover, Hants SP10 5BE, or to Routledge Inc, 29 West 35th Street, New York NY 10001, USA.

COLLOQUIAL CD-ROMs
Multimedia Language Courses

Available in: Chinese, French, Portuguese and Spanish

Colloquial
Spanish
The Complete Course for Beginners

Untza Otaola Alday

Routledge
Taylor & Francis Group

LONDON AND NEW YORK

A aita y ama

First published 1995
by Routledge
11 New Fetter Lane, London EC4P 4EE

Simultaneously published in the USA and Canada
by Routledge
29 West 35th Street, New York, NY 10001

Reprinted 1996, 1998, 1999, 2001, 2003, 2004

Routledge is an imprint of the Taylor & Francis Group

© 1995 Untza Otaola Alday

Illustrations by Ron Julien

Typeset in Times Ten by
Florence Production Ltd, Stoodleigh, Devon
Printed and bound in Great Britain by
Biddles Ltd, King's Lynn, Norfolk.

British Library Cataloguing in Publication Data
A catalogue record for this book is available from the British Library

Library of Congress Cataloguing in Publication Data
A catalog record for this book is available from the Library of Congress

ISBN 0–415–03024–2 (Book)

ISBN 0–415–03025–0 (Cassettes)

ISBN 0–415–12681–9 (CDs)

ISBN 0–415–30633–7 (Book, cassettes and CDs course)

Contents

About this book

Colloquial Spanish can be used by adult learners working with or without a teacher.

Each lesson begins with a list of things that you should be able to understand and use by the time you finish the lesson. This is followed by a 'Dialogue' with a short introduction in English. In the first five lessons you will find a list of new words you will have come across in the dialogue, followed by a full translation. However, from Lesson 6, the translation is not provided. By this stage you should be trying to understand the meaning of unfamiliar language from the context, by listening or reading for clues. Don't worry if you can't understand much to start with; you will build up a feeling for the language as you progress.

The 'Dialogues' are followed by 'Language points' where you will find explanations of many of the functional and grammar points that you have come across in the dialogue. However, don't expect to find everything explained. Some items will be explained in later lessons. You will find a number of examples that will clarify each language point covered.

The 'Language points' section is generally followed by 'Spanish culture', a short section in English which looks at different aspects of Spanish life, from types of hotels to how to rent a car. This is followed by 'Language in use', a selection of exercises that focus your attention on the items introduced in 'Language points'. When in doubt, look back at the 'Language points' section. The second part of the lesson follows the same pattern with the inclusion of a short pronunciation section.

After 'Language in use', you will find one or two exercises under 'Vocabulary building'. In this section you will learn new words and expressions either by their association with material you have already learned, or through their similarities to their English counterparts.

Each lesson ends with a 'Reading' section in which you are asked to answer some questions after reading a passage or dialogue. You will find words that you do not know. Don't worry! Try to see if you can guess the meaning of the words from the context. Often you will find that you do not need to know the precise meaning of each word in order to understand the main points.

If you're really serious about learning Spanish, you should use the tapes that accompany this book. This will make the task of pronouncing and understanding Spanish a great deal easier. Although the pronunciation of Spanish does not usually create too many problems for English speakers (with the exception of the rolled r), there are one or two things that you should know before you start.

Pronunciation guide 📼

Letter	name	pronunciation	Spanish example	English equivalent
a	a	/a/	la	hat
b	be	/b/	beber	boat
c	ce	/θ/ /k/	cero, casa	thing, case
ch	che	/ch /	coche	much
d	de	/d/ /ð/	dedo, miedo	day, this
e	e	/e/	España	bed
f	efe	/f/	fuego	France
g	ge	/g/ /x/	gato, gente	goat, loch
h	hache	–	hola	never pronounced
i	i	/i/	Italia	fit
j	jota	/x/	jamón	loch
k	ka	/k/	kilo	kilometre
l	ele	/l/	luna	last
ll	elle	/ʎ/	Sevilla	million, yes
m	eme	/m/	Madrid	mean
n	ene	/n/	no	night
ñ	eñe	/ɲ/	España	onion
o	o	/o/	oso	holiday
p	pe	/p/	pollo	pen
q	cu	/k/	queso	cat
r	ere, erre	/r/ /rr/	caro, guitarra	no equivalent
s	ese	/s/	sí	six
t	te	/t/	tío	tea
u	u	/u/	un	food

v	uve	/b/	*v*aso	*b*et
w	uve doble	/b/ /w/	*w*ater, *w*hisky	*b*at, *w*hisky
x	equis	/s/ /ks/	e*x*tra, ta*x*i	*s*ort, ta*x*i
y	i griega	/y/ /i/	*y*o, so*y*	*y*es, bo*y*
z	zeta	/θ/	*z*apato	*th*ing

The vowel sounds in Spanish are short.

Note the following points:

the vowel **u** is not pronounced in **gue, gui, que** and **qui**;
the letters **b** and **v** are pronounced in the same way: **vino** and **beso**;
the letter **h** is not pronounced: **hola**;
the letter **x** is pronounced /s/ in front of a consonant: **exterior**;
the double **r** can only go between two vowels: **perro**;
za, ce, ci, zo, zu are all pronounced with the sound /θ/.
ca, que, qui, co, cu are all pronounced with the sound /k/;
ga, gue, gui, go, gu are all pronounced with the sound /g/;
ja, je, ge, ji, gi, jo, ju are all pronounced with the sound /x/.

1 Encuentros

Meeting people

In this lesson we will look at:

- simple introductions, enquiries and greetings
- gender (masculine and feminine)
- basic adjective use
- the verbs **ser** and **estar**

Throughout this course you will see that many words in Spanish are similar to English words. There are others where you will be able to guess the meaning from the root. To begin with, see if you can match the following countries to their nationalities:

América	argentino(a)
Francia	inglés(a)
Brasil	español(a)
Méjico	francés(a)
Inglaterra	brasileño(a)
Argentina	mejicano(a)
España	americano(a)
Australia	canadiense
Canada	australiano(a)

Dialogue 🔲

Meeting the family

Laura, a Spanish student, decides to spend some time with a Spanish family who were recommended by a friend. She goes to meet the family

LAURA: ¡Hola! Buenos días. Soy Laura.

TERESA:	¡Claro! Hola Laura, yo soy Teresa, la hermana de Carmen.
	Pero pasa, por favor. ¿Cómo estás? ¿Qué tal el viaje?
LAURA:	Muy bien, gracias.
TERESA:	¿Estás cansada?
LAURA:	Un poco.

LAURA:	*Hello! Good morning. I'm Laura.*
TERESA:	*Of course! Hello Laura, I'm Teresa, Carmen's sister. Come in. How are you? How was the journey?*
LAURA:	*Very good, thank you.*
TERESA:	*Are you tired?*
LAURA:	*A little bit.*

Vocabulary

hola	hello	**cómo**	how
buenos días	good morning	**estás**	(you) are
soy	(I) am	**qué tal**	what about
¡claro!	of course! (literally 'clear')	**el**	the
la	the	**el viaje**	journey
hermana	sister	**muy**	very
de	of	**bien**	well
pero	but	**gracias**	thanks
pasa	come in	**cansada(o)**	tired
por favor	please	**un poco**	a little

Language points

Introductions using ser: 'to be'

You may have noticed from the first dialogue that there is no need to use the subject pronoun (e.g. I, you, etc.) in Spanish. The ending of the verb tells the listener who you are referring to.

Soy **Laura**	*I am* Laura
¿Eres **Carmen?**	*Are you* Carmen?
Es **Juan**	*He is* John

However, if you want to emphasize whom you are talking about, or talking to, you should use the full form. That is, use the subject pronoun (i.e. **yo, tú, él,** etc.).

Yo **soy la hermana de Carmen**	*I* am Carmen's sister
Tú **eres Carmen ¿no?**	*You* are Carmen, aren't you?
El **es el hermano de María**	*He* is María's brother
Ella **es la madre de Carmen**	*She* is Carmen's mother

Yes/no questions are questions to which the answer could be a simple yes or no. Notice that the word order does not change in yes/no questions.

¿Eres Carmen?	Are you Carmen?
¿Eres la hermana de Carmen?	Are you Carmen's sister?

¿ ? , ¡ ! and ´

In spoken Spanish, the intonation signals a question, as in English.

In written Spanish, an inverted question mark is used at the beginning of a question as well as the usual question mark at the end. In addition, Spanish uses an inverted exclamation mark at the beginning of an exclamation as well as the usual exclamation mark at the end.

¡Qué bonito!	How pretty!
¡Qué caro!	How expensive!

You will have noticed that certain words like **tú** and **él** have accents. These monosyllabic words (words with one sound) need an accent in order to distinguish them from other words that have the same spelling.

Tú **eres Carmen ¿no?**	*You* are Carmen, aren't you?
Tu **hermana es Carmen ¿no?**	*Your* sister is Carmen, isn't she?
Él **es Juan**	*He* is Juan
El **viaje**	*The* journey

In addition, words like **que** have an accent when they are used in questions and exclamations.

¿*Qué* tal el viaje?	*How* was the journey?
¡*Qué* caro!	*How* expensive!

Masculine and feminine

A noun is a word that refers to people, things or abstract qualities (e.g. house, Carmen, trust). Nouns in Spanish are either masculine or feminine, so there are two words for 'the', according to whether the noun is masculine or feminine. The word **el** is used for masculine nouns and **la** for feminine nouns. Most words ending in **o** are masculine whilst those ending in **a** are generally feminine.

la hermana	the sister	**el viaje**	the journey
el hermano	the brother	**la noche**	the night

However, as there are some exceptions to the rule, you should learn new words with their respective articles (**el**, **la**).

la radio	the radio	**el tema**	the topic
la foto	the photo	**el problema**	the problem

'To be'

There are two verbs in Spanish corresponding to the English verb 'to be'. You will discover later some of the contexts in which they are used. For the moment the most important distinction between them is that the verb **ser** refers to something which is permanent (like your name) while the verb **estar** refers to temporary conditions (like being tired).

Soy Carlos	I am Carlos
Carlos es de Bilbao	Carlos is from Bilbao
Estoy cansada	I am tired
¿Estás cansado?	Are you tired?
Pedro está ocupado	Pedro is busy

Adjectives in Spanish

Adjectives are words that describe a quality (e.g. big, blue, boring). You saw in the dialogue and in the examples given above that the adjective **cansado(a)** agrees with the gender (masculine or feminine) of the noun it refers to.

Está ocupada	She is busy	(**a** for feminine)
Está ocupado	He is busy	(**o** for masculine)

Note that adjectives ending in 'e' do not change according to gender.

Está libre	S/he is free

The informal tú

Tú, meaning you, is the form of address that would normally be used by young people, between friends and in informal situations. Later in the book you will learn other more formal ways of addressing people.

Greetings

la tarde	afternoon
la noche	night
hola	hello: can be used at any time of the day.

Notice that in Spanish you often use two greetings, **hola** followed by, for example, **buenos días**.

Buenos días	good morning (literally 'good days').
Buenas tardes	good afternoon (used after about 2 p.m.)
Buenas noches	good evening, good night.

You can use **buenas noches** to greet someone as well as when you leave them (used after dusk).

Once you have greeted the person you should ask:

¿Cómo estás?   How are you?

¿Qué tal?   How are you? (or How are things?) A little more informal than **¿cómo estás?**

And you may reply to both of them:

Muy bien, gracias   I'm fine (very well), thanks

And to enquire about somebody else:

¿Cómo está tu hermana?   How is your sister?

Bien, gracias   Fine, thanks

We saw **¿qué tal?** used on its own to mean 'how are you?'. You can use it in the same way to refer to other people and situations:

¿Qué tal tu hermana?   How is your sister?

¿Qué tal el viaje?   How was the journey?

Exercise 1

How would these people introduce themselves?

1 Brian, Max's brother
2 Stella, Laura's sister
3 Carmen, Teresa's sister
4 Teresa, Juan's sister
5 Juan, Teresa's brother
6 Claudio, Juan's brother

Exercise 2

You are at a party and you confuse each of the above people with their brother/sister. Write your question and their reply.

   e.g. Hola, ¿eres Max?
         No, soy Brian, el hermano de Max.

Exercise 3

You need some help from your Spanish friend. How would you ask him if:

1 he is tired/busy/ill/free
2 his brother is tired/busy/free/ill
3 his sister is tired/busy/ill/free

(Note: **enfermo(a)** ill.)

Exercise 4

y   and
mi   my

Our Spanish friend wants some help. How do you tell her:

1 that you are busy but your sister is free
2 that you are tired but your brother is not busy
3 that you are free but your sister is ill
4 that your brother is not free and you are ill
5 that you are busy and your sister is tired

Exercise 5

Ask Carmen how these people are:

1 Max
2 her sister, Teresa
3 her brother, Pedro
4 Juan's brother
5 Laura's sister

Now give Carmen's replies.

Exercise 6

Use **qué tal** to ask someone about:

1 the journey
2 the film (**la película**) he saw
3 the party (**la fiesta**)
4 his sister

Exercise 7

Rewrite the dialogue at the beginning of this section so that it takes place between Max and Claudio at night.

Dialogue 🔘

Introductions

Teresa introduces Laura to some members of her family

TERESA: ¡Hola, Carmen! ¡Mira!, ésta es Laura, la amiga inglesa de John.
CARMEN: Encantada, Laura.
LAURA: Mucho gusto.
TERESA: Y ésta es mamá.
MADRE: Encantada, bienvenida a nuestra casa.
LAURA: Muchas gracias.
PEDRO: Y yo soy Pedro, el hermano de estas dos.
LAURA: Encantada.

TERESA: *Hello Carmen. Look, this is Laura, John's English friend.*
CARMEN: *Pleased to meet you, Laura.*
LAURA: *Pleased to meet you.*
TERESA: *And this is (our) mum.*
MOTHER: *Pleased to meet you, welcome to our house.*
LAURA: *Thank you very much.*
PEDRO: *And I am the brother of these two.*
LAURA: *Pleased to meet you.*

Vocabulary

¡mira!	look!	**mamá**	mum
ésta	this (female) (pronoun)	**bienvenida(o)**	welcome (it takes the gender of the person you are saying it to)
amiga(o)	friend	**a**	to
inglés(a)	English	**nuestra(o)**	our (it takes the gender of the object)
encantada(o)	pleased to meet you	**la casa**	house
mucho gusto	pleased to meet you	**estas**	these (female) (adjective)

Language points

Gender of adjectives

español Spanish

We have met two adjectives (**cansado** and **ocupado**) where the final -**o** of the masculine form is replaced by -**a** in the feminine form. Other adjectives add -**a** to the masculine form to make the feminine:

Masculine	*Feminine*	
argentino	**argentina**	*but*
inglés	**inglesa**	
español	**española**	

You will have noticed that the masculine form (**inglés**) has an accent on the **é** whilst the feminine form does not. When the masculine form ends in **s** or **n** then the final vowel has an accent. Notice that adjectives of nationality do not have capital letters.

Soy inglesa	I am English
Es australiano	He is Australian

Notice also that the adjective follows the noun it modifies:

mi amiga inglesa	my English friend
mi coche español	my Spanish car

Introducing people more formally

Éste es mi amigo, Pedro	This is my friend, Pedro
Ésta es Carmen, mi hermana	This is Carmen, my sister

Pronunciation 🔊

The letter 'h' is not pronounced at all in Spanish. Practise:

hola   **hermano**   **hasta**   **hora**

Language in use

Exercise 8

Introduce the following people formally:

1 Arantxa's mother
2 Carmen's brother
3 José's sister
4 Carmen's father
5 Sonia's Spanish friend, Carmen

Exercise 9

el jefe   boss

You arrive at a Spanish party with your brother and your boss and you have to introduce everyone to your hostess. Write a dialogue of what you would say.

Exercise 10

Give true answers to these questions:

1 ¿Estás cansado(a)?
2 ¿Eres inglés/inglesa?
3 ¿Estás ocupado(a)?
4 ¿Eres tú el amigo/la amiga de Carmen?
5 ¿Es John tu hermano?

Exercise 11

Match the pairs to make an appropriate response to each statement or question on the left:

1 ¿Estás ocupada?   (a) Encantado
2 ¿Cómo estás?   (b) Sí, es Elena
3 ¿Eres María?   (c) muy bien, gracias
4 Encantada   (d) no, soy Teresa
5 ¿Es la amiga de Juan?   (e) muy bien, gracias
6 Éste es mi hermano   (f) no mucho
7 Bienvenido a mi casa   (g) mucho gusto
8 ¿Qué tal el viaje?   (h) muchas gracias

Exercise 12

A Spanish friend of yours is confused about the nationality of some celebrities. Tell her whether she is right or wrong.

1 Madonna es inglesa ¿no?
2 El jugador de tenis Pat Cash es inglés ¿no?
3 El actor Sean Connery es americano ¿no?
4 La cantante Sade es americana ¿no?
5 La película 'El Piano' es canadiense ¿no?
6 El actor Daniel Day Lewis es irlandés ¿no?

Vocabulary building

Exercise 13

Find out the masculine or feminine form of the following nationalities:

1 francés   _____
2 americano   _____
3 _____   argentina
4 brasileño   _____
5 _____   mejicana
6 canadiense   _____
7 irlandés   _____
8 _____   escocesa

Exercise 14

Which is the odd word out?

inglesa, española, ocupado, enferma
hermano, hermana, papá, vale
oficina, bar, maleta, aeropuerto
cansado, jefe, enfermo, libre
viaje, aeropuerto, coche, casa
noche, película, día, tarde

Exercise 15

Many words in Spanish are formed by adding different endings to the same root. Other words can be made by combining words. The words below are all similar to words you have learnt in this lesson. Can you guess their meaning by matching them to an English word on the right?

1 viajero   (a) illness
2 puerto   (b) occupy
3 enfermedad   (c) travel
4 libertad   (d) traveller
5 amistad   (e) freedom
6 viajar   (f) friendship
7 ocupar   (g) port
8 enfermera   (h) nurse

Reading

An American friend of María's brother is coming to Spain to spend some time with María's family. María went to meet him at the airport. While you are reading, try to find out the following:

1 Who is María with?
2 How was Peter's journey?
3 Where are they going?

En el aeropuerto

MARÍA: Disculpa, ¿eres Peter?
PETER: Sí, ¿y tú?
MARÍA: Soy la hermana de José, y éste es mi amigo Javier.
PETER: Encantado.
JAVIER: Mucho gusto. Bienvenido a Madrid.
PETER: Gracias.
MARÍA: ¿Qué tal el viaje?
PETER: Muy bien, gracias.
JAVIER: ¿Y la película?
MARÍA: Mira, Javier. Peter debe de estar muy cansado. Vamos a casa. ¿Es ésta tu maleta?
PETER: Sí, ésta.
MARÍA: Vamos pues a casa.

Vocabulary

disculpa   excuse me
la maleta   suitcase
vamos pues   let's go, then

2 ¿De dónde eres?

Where are you from?

In this lesson we will look at:

- talking about likes and dislikes
- the present tense of **-ar** verbs
- more uses of **ser** and **estar**
- negative sentences
- the numbers 1 to 20

Dialogue 🔲

Asking where people come from

Laura and Carmen are going to a party given by Manolo, one of Carmen's friends

MANOLO: ¡Hola Carmen! ¿Qué tal?
CARMEN: Muy bien. Mira Manolo, ésta es Laura.
MANOLO: Encantado.
LAURA: Hola Manolo.
MANOLO: ¿De dónde eres? No eres española ¿verdad?
LAURA: No, soy inglesa, de Londres. Y tú ¿de dónde eres?
MANOLO: De Huelva.
LAURA: ¿Huelva? ¿Dónde está?
MANOLO: En el sur de España.
LAURA: ¡Ah! Por eso el acento.

MANOLO: *Hello Carmen! How are things?*
CARMEN: *Very good. Look Manolo, this is Laura.*
MANOLO: *Pleased to meet you.*
LAURA: *Hello Manolo.*
MANOLO: *Where are you from? You aren't Spanish, are you?*

LAURA: *No, I am English, from London. And you, where are you from?*
MANOLO: *From Huelva.*
LAURA: *Huelva? Where is that?*
MANOLO: *In the south of Spain.*
LAURA: *Ah! That's why you have an accent!*

Vocabulary

¿verdad? are you? (literally 'truth')
el sur the south
por eso that's why
el acento accent

Language points

Asking where people are from

Ser de *(to be from)*

¿De dónde eres?	Where are you from?
Soy de Zaragoza	I am from Zaragoza
¿De dónde es Julio?	Where is Julio from?
Es de Galicia	He is from Galicia
Felipe González es de Sevilla	Felipe González is from Seville

Notice that the preposition **de** goes at the beginning of the question, but after the verb when it is in the answer.

Expressing location

Estar

We are going to look at another use of the verb **estar**. **Estar** is used for talking about where places or people are.

Estoy en casa	I am at home
¿Dónde estás?	Where are you?
El hotel está en el centro	The hotel is in the centre
Bilbao está en el norte de España	Bilbao is in the north of Spain

Granada está en el sur de España	Granada is in the south of Spain
Cáceres está en el oeste de España	Cáceres is in the west of Spain
Alicante está en el este de España	Alicante is in the east of Spain

Note that the preposition **en** is used regardless of whether the prepositions 'in' or 'at' are used in English.

Forming negative sentences

You will probably have noticed in the dialogue that the negative is formed by placing **no** before the verb.

No **eres española ¿verdad?**	You are *not* Spanish, are you?
Zaragoza *no* **está en el sur**	Zaragoza is *not* in the south
Sonia *no* **está en casa**	Sonia is *not* at home

This rule applies to all verbs in all the tenses.

No **hablo español**	I do *not* speak Spanish
No **he hablado con Juan**	I have *not* spoken to Juan

More on masculine and feminine

We saw in the previous chapter that the word for 'the' is **el** for masculine nouns and **la** for feminine nouns. These words apply to nouns referring to a specific person or thing, e.g. **la hermana de Juan**. However, when you want to refer to a person or thing, but not to any specific one, you must use the word **un** in front of a masculine word and **una** in front of a feminine one.

Vocabulary

una amiga	a female friend
un amigo	a male friend
una casa	a house
un viaje	a journey

Spanish culture

Spain is divided into 17 autonomous communities, but not all of them have political autonomy. Spanish is the official language, but there are in fact four main languages spoken in the peninsula: **español** (Spanish), **catalán** (Catalan), **vasco/euskera** (Basque), and **gallego** (Galician). There are also regional dialects such as **aragonés** and **andaluz**. Accents vary according to the region.

Language in use

Exercise 1

You have been advised to visit certain places in Spain. You do not know where they are so you have to ask a Spanish friend. Ask where the following places are:

1 Toledo   4 Santander
2 Valencia   5 Vitoria
3 Jaén   6 Tarragona

Exercise 2

Mapa de España: look at the map below and say where the places listed in exercise 1 are.

Exercise 3

You need to get hold of a few people as you are planning a party. Ask a friend where five of your other friends are. Write out the reply as well.

e.g. ¿Está Luisa en Madrid?
No, está en Salamanca

Exercise 4

You have been invited to a party attended by people from all the EC countries. Ask them where they are from. An example is provided for you:

– ¿De dónde eres?
– Soy de Italia. ¿Y tú?
– Soy de Inglaterra.

Exercise 5

If you have the cassettes, listen and find out where each person is from.

Exercise 6

Give a negative answer to the following questions:

1 ¿Eres de España?
2 ¿Está Bilbao en el sur de España?
3 ¿Estás cansada/o?
4 ¿Está tu madre en casa?
5 ¿Eres Lola?
6 ¿Hablas alemán?

Dialogue

Likes and dislikes

Manolo wants to know what Laura thinks of Spain

MANOLO: ¿Qué te parece España? ¿Te gusta?
LAURA: Sólo llevo aquí cinco días pero sí, me gusta mucho.
MANOLO: ¿Es ésta la primera vez que visitas España?
LAURA: Sí, la primera.
MANOLO: Pues hablas muy bien el español.
LAURA: Gracias.

MANOLO: *What do you think of Spain? Do you like it?*
LAURA: *I have only been here for five days but yes, I like it a lot.*
MANOLO: *Is this the first time you have visited Spain?*
LAURA: *Yes, the first (time).*
MANOLO: *Well, you speak Spanish really well.*
LAURA: *Thanks.*

Vocabulary

te parece	you think
te gusta	you like
sólo	only
llevo	I have been (literally 'I take')
aquí	here
cinco	five
días	days (it is a masculine word: **el día**)
primera(o)	first
vez	time (not for the clock)
visitas	you visit
sí	yes
pues	an expression; here it could be translated as 'well'
hablas	you speak

Language points

You will probably have noticed that the verb endings change according to the person they refer to. Although there are some irregularities, most endings in the present tense are the same. Verbs in Spanish are divided into three groups according to their infinitive (that is, base form) endings. These infinitive endings are:

	-ar	**-er**	**-ir**
Example:	habl*ar*	com*er*	viv*ir*

Here are the 'I', 'you' and 'he/she/it' present tense endings for the **-ar** regular verbs that have appeared in the dialogue.

Habl*o* español y francés	I speak Spanish and French
Habl*as* español muy bien	You speak Spanish very well
John habl*a* español	John speaks Spanish

Llev*o* en España tres días	I have been in Spain for three days
¿Llev*as* mucho tiempo aquí?	¿Have you been here long?
Bob llev*a* aquí dos días	Bob has been here two days

Notice that in order to express the time, starting in the past and lasting up until now that you have been in a place, Spanish uses the present tense of **llevar**.

Gustar *(to like)*

The verb **gustar** does not follow the pattern outlined above. It is formed like the English verb 'to please'. Note that it must go with its indirect pronoun (we will look at them further on in the book) according to the person it refers to (e.g. me, you, them, etc.)

Me gusta España	I like Spain (*or* Spain pleases me)
¿Te gusta Madrid?	Do you like Madrid? (*or* Does Madrid please you?)
No **le gusta** Sevilla	S/he does not like Seville (*or* Seville doesn't please her/him)

Note that the negative adverb **no** goes before the indirect object.

The endings of the verb do not change with the person doing the liking, as you have seen with other verbs. The endings of the verb change according to the number, i.e. singular and plural, of the object/person that is liked:

Me *gusta* España	I like Spain
Me *gustan* los españoles	I like the Spanish people
No me *gusta* esta casa	I don't like this house
Me *gustan* estos pueblos	I like these villages

Note that the verb **parecer** that appears in the dialogue is formed like the verb **gustar**. Therefore the endings of the verb do not change.

Me parece bien	I think it is good
¿Te parece bien?	Do you think it is OK?
Le parece mal	S/he disagrees / s/he doesn't like the idea

Pues

Pues is often used in spoken Spanish, and although it has many different uses, there are two that should be learnt as they will be very useful in conversation. You saw one of these uses in the previous dialogue, when Manolo begins his response with **pues** as a consequence of what Laura had said. One of its uses, therefore, is as an immediate response to another comment.

Sólo llevo aquí cuatro días	I have only been here for four days
Pues estás muy morena	Well (that being so), you are very tanned

Pues is often used when there is hesitation on the part of the speaker. You'll find this very useful while you are learning as it will give you time to think of an answer.

¿Dónde está tu hermano?	Where is your brother?
Pues no sé	Well, I don't know

Numbers

Here are the numbers up to 20.

1	uno/a	11	once
2	dos	12	doce
3	tres	13	trece
4	cuatro	14	catorce
5	cinco	15	quince
6	seis	16	dieciséis
7	siete	17	diecisiete
8	ocho	18	dieciocho
9	nueve	19	diecinueve
10	diez	20	veinte

You have probably noticed that numbers 16–19 combine **diez y seis** ('ten' and 'six'), **diez y siete**, etc.

uno/a *takes the gender of the noun*

una **casa**	one house
un **coche**	one car

Notice that **uno** loses its final **o** in front of a masculine noun:

Llevo *un* día en Bilbao	I have been in Bilbao for one day
Llevo *un* año en Salamanca	I have been in Salamanca for one year

Pronunciation 🔘

In the first dialogue of this lesson you were introduced to the province of Huelva. By now you know that the letter **h** is not pronounced in Spanish. However, when the **h** is followed by **ue**, the **h** is pronounced as a soft **g**.

Huelva **está en Andalucía**	Huelva is in Andalucía
No me gustan los *huevos*	I do not like eggs
Pedro está en *huelga*	Pedro is on strike

Language in use

Exercise 7

Answer the following questions using **Sí** or **No**:

1 ¿Hablas francés?
2 ¿Hablas italiano?
3 ¿Eres australiano/a?
4 ¿Te gusta el español?
5 ¿Te gustan los españoles?
6 ¿Te gustan las películas francesas?

Exercise 8

Answer the following questions

1 ¿Hablas alemán o francés?
2 ¿Eres americano o australiano?
3 ¿Te gusta el español o el francés?
4 ¿Te gustan las películas francesas o las españolas?

Exercise 9

Answer the following questions:

lenguas   languages

1 ¿Qué lenguas hablas?
2 ¿De dónde eres?
3 ¿Qué lenguas te gustan?
4 ¿Qué películas te gustan?

Vocabulary building

Exercise 10

Match the following numbers:

1	treinta	(a)	90
2	ochenta	(b)	70
3	cuarenta	(c)	30
4	noventa	(d)	80
5	cincuenta	(e)	40
6	setenta	(f)	50
7	sesenta	(g)	60

Exercise 11

Here are some of the Spanish regions. Try to match the region with the name given to the people who live there:

1	Cataluña	(a)	riojano/a
2	Galicia	(b)	madrileño/a
3	Euskadi (País Vasco)	(c)	catalán/catalana
4	La Rioja	(d)	andaluz/andaluza
5	Madrid	(e)	vasco/a
6	Andalucía	(f)	gallego/a

Reading

Read the following description.

Chuck es un norteamericano que lleva en Madrid diez días en casa de una amiga española. Chuck habla inglés, francés y un poco de español. Le gusta mucho España pero ésta es la primera vez que está aquí. Quiere hablar español bien y por eso estudia todos los días.

Are the following statements **verdadero** (true) or **falso** (false)?

1 Chuck es de los Estados Unidos
2 Chuck lleva en España once días
3 Chuck está con una amiga española
4 Ésta no es la primera vez que visita España
5 Chuck no habla alemán

Now see if you can write similar facts about yourself.

3 ¡Taxi!

Taking a cab

> In this lesson we will look at:
>
> - Prices and quantities
> - the verbs **tener**, **ir** and **venir**
> - the present tense of **-er** and **-ir** verbs
> - the numbers 21 to 90

Dialogue

To the hotel

Michael, a businessman from Australia, is in Barajas airport in Madrid. He needs to get to his hotel

MICHAEL: ¡Taxi!
TAXISTA: ¿Adónde va, señor?
MICHAEL: Al Hotel Excelsior, por favor.
TAXISTA: Bien, ¿es ésa su maleta?
MICHAEL: Sí y ésta también.
TAXISTA: Vale. ¿De dónde viene?
MICHAEL: De Australia.
TAXISTA: ¿Es australiano?
MICHAEL: Sí.
TAXISTA: ¿Vive por casualidad en Sydney?
MICHAEL: Sí, ¿lo conoce?
TAXISTA: Sí, mi hermano vive allí.

MICHAEL: *Taxi!*
TAXISTA: *Where are you going, sir?*

MICHAEL: *To the Excelsior Hotel, please.*
TAXISTA: *Fine. Is that your suitcase?*
MICHAEL: *Yes, and this one too.*
TAXISTA: *OK. Where do you come from?*
MICHAEL: *From Australia.*
TAXISTA: *Are you Australian?*
MICHAEL: *Yes.*
TAXISTA: *Do you by any chance live in Sydney?*
MICHAEL: *Yes, do you know it?*
TAXISTA: *Yes, my brother lives there.*

Vocabulary

va	you go (formal)
señor	sir
por favor	please
también	also
viene	you come (formal)
vive	you live (formal)
por casualidad	by chance
sí	yes
lo	it (it refers to masculine words)
conoce	you know (formal)
allí	there

Language points

Ir *(to go)*

Ir is an irregular verb.

Voy **a la cafetería, ¿vienes?**	I am *going* to the coffee shop, are you coming?
¿Vas **a Alicante esta tarde?**	Are *you going* to Alicante this afternoon?
Luis *va* **al cine luego**	Luis *is going* to the cinema later
¿Vas **al banco hoy?**	Are *you going* to the bank today?

You will probably have noticed that the preposition 'a' joins the article **el** to form a single word, **al**, but it does not join the feminine article **la**.

¿Vas *al* supermercado hoy?	Are you going *to the* supermarket today?
¿Vas *a la* embajada mañana?	Are you going *to the* embassy tomorrow?

Notice as well that the preposition **a** goes at the beginning of an open question. Although you will normally see **a** forming one single word with **donde**, there will be occasions when you will see it as two separate words as this is becoming more common.

¿*Adónde* vas esta noche?	Where are you going tonight?
¿*A dónde* vas mañana?	Where are you going tomorrow?

In English you use the present continous form ('I am going') rather than 'I go', whilst in Spanish the present form is used. It is better not to use the present continous of the verb '**ir**' as it is rarely used.

You can use **ir** followed by **a** in a future sense, to talk of future plans. Here, this is the equivalent of the English 'going to':

***Voy a* comer con el señor Pérez**	*I am going to* eat with Mr Perez
¿*Vas a* ver a Carmen?	Are *you going to* see Carmen?
***Va a* salir esta noche**	S/he *is going to* leave tonight

Verbs that end in **-er** have the following endings:

Beber *(to drink)*

Normalmente beb*o* vino	*I* normally *drink* wine.
¿Beb*es* vino con las comidas?	Do *you drink* wine with meals?
Pedro no beb*e* nada alcohólico	Pedro does not *drink* alcohol

These endings are the same for the verbs that end in **-ir**.

Vivir *(to live)*

Viv*o* en el centro	*I live* in the centre (of town).
¿Viv*es* en Nueva York?	Do *you live* in New York?
Víctor viv*e* en Lugo	*Víctor lives* in Lugo.

Demonstratives

We used **ésta** in the previous lesson for introducing people:

Ésta es Concha   *This* is Concha

Below is a list of some other Spanish demonstratives:

ésta/esta, éste/este, ésa/esa, ése/ese, aquél/aquel, aquélla/aquella

When they are used on their own the **esta** words only have an accent on the first 'e' to distinguish them from the verb form **está**:

Me gusta *ésta*   I like *this one* (referring to a feminine object)

Me gusta *éste*   I like *this one* (referring to a masculine object)

However, notice what happens when used with a noun:

Me gusta *este coche*   I like *this car*
Me gusta *esta película*   I like *this film*

The words **éste** and **este** change in the plural form to **éstos** and **estos**, whilst **esta** just takes an **s**.

Me gustan *estos coches*   I like *these cars*
¿Te gustan *estas películas*?   Do you like *these films*?

When the object is not right next to the speaker then the words **ese** and **esa** are used instead of **este** and **esta**.

Ese coche es muy rápido   *That car* is very fast
Esa casa es muy cara   *That house* is very expensive
Ésa me gusta más   I like *that one* more

In addition, Spanish makes a further distinction according to the distance between the speakers and the object they are referring to. When the object is far from both speakers, then the words **aquel** and **aquella** are used.

Aquel coche es muy lento   *That car* is very slow
Aquella casa es muy barata   *That house* is very cheap
Aquélla es más barata   *That one* is cheaper

Venir de *(to come from)*

This verb is irregular. However, the endings of the verb are the same as for all the other verbs that end in **-ir**. Remember that these are the same as for **-er** verbs.

Vengo **de Jaén**	I (have) come from Jaén
¿Vienes **de casa?**	Have you come from home?
José viene **hoy de Almería**	José is coming from Almería today

Venir de is not used in Spanish to mean the place of origin, but to mean where the person has just come from.

Vengo de **Londres pero soy australiano**	*I have just come* from London but I am Australian

Remember that the preposition **de** goes in front of the particle **dónde**:

¿De dónde vienes?	Where do you come from?
¿De dónde viene Juan?	Where does Juan come from?

More numbers

21	veintiuno/a	31	treinta y uno/a
22	veintidós	32	treinta y dos
23	veintitrés	40	cuarenta
24	veinticuatro	41	cuarenta y uno/a
25	veinticinco	50	cincuenta
26	veintiséis	51	cincuenta y uno/a
27	veintisiete	60	sesenta
28	veintiocho	70	setenta
29	veintinueve	80	ochenta
30	treinta	90	noventa

Note that **veinte** becomes **veinti** plus the number. However, all the other numbers have three separate words although they are said so fast that they may sound like one word. The numbers **seis** (6) and **siete** (7) lose their 'i' when they form **sesenta** and **setenta**.

The formal usted

Usted is the form of address that would normally be used with strangers and to show respect, particularly to the speaker's elders.

Although its use is declining, it is still used by a large number of people.

When you need to use this form, take the third person singular of the verb and use it instead of the second, which is used with **tú**. Go back to the dialogue and see which form of address the taxi driver is using.

¿Cómo está usted?	How are you?
¿Habla usted español?	Do you speak Spanish?
¿A usted le gusta el trabajo?	Do you like the job?

You will see the form **usted** in the abbreviated forms **Vd.** or **Ud.** However, its pronunciation remains the same as in **usted**.

¿Tiene Vd. una habitación doble?	Do you have a double room?

Spanish culture

There are many different types of places to stay in Spain. The cheapest of all are **Fondas** (F) which are normally situated above a bar, followed closely by **Casas de Huéspedes** (CH) and **Pensiones** (P). Slightly more expensive are **Hostales (Hs)** which are categorized with one to three stars. **Hoteles (H)** also have star ratings up to five stars. In addition, the state-run **Paradores** are beautiful places to stay as they are often converted castles and monasteries. Although some of the **paradores** are quite expensive, many of them offer very good value. You can get a list of the paradores of the region you are intending to visit from the tourist office. All prices are fixed by the **precio de tablilla** (tariff) published annually by the official hotel guide and compiled by the **Secretaría General de Turismo**.

If you are not happy with your room or you think you have been overcharged, you can ask for the **Libro de Reclamaciones** (complaints book) which, by law, all establishments must keep.

Language in use

Exercise 1

Fill in the appropriate term: **al** or **a la**. (Note **la playa** the beach.)

1 Esta noche voy _____ teatro.
2 Mañana voy _____ playa.
3 ¿Vas _____ piscina mañana?
4 Esta semana voy _____ oficina de Salamanca.
5 ¿Vas _____ bar ahora?
6 Esta noche Pedro va _____ restaurante.

Exercise 2

You are with five Spanish friends. You do not know what to do in the evening so you ask everyone where they are going to help you decide. Write your questions with their answers.

> e.g.   ¿Adónde vas esta noche?
>   Voy al cine.

Exercise 3

Fill in the appropriate form of the verb **ir**:

1 Mañana _____ al centro (Yo)
2 ¿Adónde _____ Pedro mañana?
3 ¿Adónde _____ esta noche? (Tú)
4 Hoy _____ a estudiar mucho (Yo)
5 Manolo no _____ hoy, _____ mañana.

Exercise 4

Fill in the gaps using **este**, **éste**, **esta** and **ésta**

1 No me gusta _____ coche
2 ¿Es _____ tu amigo?
3 _____ radio es muy moderna
4 _____ casa no es cara
5 _____ es mi hermana Elvira

Exercise 5

Match the pairs to make an appropriate response to each statement or question on the left.

1	¿Es éste tu coche?	(a)	a un restaurante italiano
2	¿Dónde está el hotel?	(b)	mucho gusto
3	¿Vas al teatro esta noche?	(c)	no, es ése
4	¿A dónde vas?	(d)	muy bien, gracias
5	Éste es mi padre	(e)	en el centro
6	¿Qué tal?	(f)	no, voy mañana

Exercise 6

You are having dinner with five colleagues from work. You have a car so you want to know if any of them live in your area so that you can give them a lift. Write the question and an appropriate response.

> e.g. A: ¿Dónde vives? ¿Vives cerca del centro?
> B: No, vivo en el norte.

Dialogue ▭

At the hotel

Michael enquires about a room in the Hotel Excelsior

RECEPCIONISTA: Buenas tardes, señor.
MICHAEL: Hola, buenas tardes. ¿Tiene una habitación individual por favor?
RECEPCIONISTA: Tiene suerte. Queda una en el primer piso. ¿Para cuántas noches?
MICHAEL: Tres o cuatro, no estoy seguro.
RECEPCIONISTA: Está bien.
MICHAEL: ¿Tiene cuarto de baño?
RECEPCIONISTA: Sí señor, todas las habitaciones tienen cuarto de baño.
MICHAEL: ¿Cuánto cuesta?
RECEPCIONISTA: Setenta y cinco euros por noche con el desayuno incluído.
MICHAEL: Muy bien, gracias.

RECEPCIONISTA: *Good afternoon, sir.*
MICHAEL: *Good afternoon. Do you have a single room please?*
RECEPCIONISTA: *You are lucky. There is one left on the first floor. For how many nights?*
MICHAEL: *Three or four, I am not sure.*
RECEPCIONISTA: *That's all right.*
MICHAEL: *Does it have a bathroom?*
RECEPCIONISTA: *Yes, all the rooms have private bathrooms.*
MICHAEL: *How much does it cost?*
RECEPCIONISTA: *Seventy five euros per night with breakfast included.*
MICHAEL: *That's fine, thanks.*

Vocabulary

tiene	you have (formal)	**piso**	floor, or flat
(la) habitación	room	**(el) cuarto de baño**	bathroom
individual	single (for rooms)	**todas**	all (feminine)
suerte	luck	**tienen**	they have
queda	there is . . . left	**¿cuánto cuesta?**	how much does it cost?
para	for	**mil**	thousand
cuántas	how many (feminine because of **(la) noche**)	**por noche**	per night
o	or	**con**	with
hay	there is/there are	**(el) desayuno**	breakfast
el primer	the first	**incluído**	inclusive

Language points

Tener *(to have)*

This verb is irregular but follows the same pattern as the verb **venir**.

Tengo **tres hermanos**	*I have* three brothers
¿Tienes **hermanas?**	Do *you have* sisters?
Valentín *tiene* **mucho dinero**	Valentín *has* a lot of money

Note that the verb **tener** is used with the meaning 'to have got', and cannot be used when the verb 'to have' is an auxiliary (i.e. a help) verb, as in 'I have finished.'

¿Cuánto . . . ?

When you want to know the price of something use **cuánto** in the singular plus the verb.

¿Cuánto cuesta ese bolso?	How much does that handbag cost?
¿Cuánto es?	How much is it?
¿Cuánto dinero tienes?	How much money do you have?

However, when you want to know about the quantity of something then **cuánto** takes the plural form and, in addition, takes the gender of the noun.

¿Cuántos hermanos tienes?	How many brothers do you have?
¿Cuántas habitaciones tienes?	How many rooms do you have?
¿Cuántas lenguas hablas?	How many languages do you speak?
¿Cuántos kilos quiere usted?	How many kilograms do you (formal) want?

Plural forms

You will have noticed that in order to form the plural of nouns and adjectives ending in **-o**, **-a**, or **-e**, an **s** is added.

El amigo de Juan es guapo	Juan's friend is handsome
Los amigos de Juan son guapos	Juan's friends are handsome
La hermana de Pedro es alta	Pedro's sister is tall
Las hermanas de Pedro son altas	Pedro's sisters are tall
El hijo de Lola es inteligente	Lola's son is intelligent
Los hijos de Lola son inteligentes	Lola's sons are intelligent

Nouns and adjectives ending in a consonant form their plurals by adding **-es**.

La ciudad es bonita	The city is pretty
Las ciudades son bonitas	Cities are pretty

Pronunciation ▣

There is no difference in Spanish between the sounds **v** and **b**; both are pronounced as a **b**.

   vivo vino bebe vaso barco vela

If you have the cassettes, listen to the following:

  Bebe muchos vasos de vino al día
  Vive en un barco de vela

Language in use

Exercise 7

Change the following informal conversations so that they apply to a more formal occasion:

1 LOLA: ¿Cómo estás?
    JAMIE: Muy bien, y ¿tú?
    LOLA: Un poco cansada, pero bien.

2 PABLO: ¿De dónde eres?
    EDMUND: De Edimburgo, y ¿tú?
    PABLO: De Cuenca.

3 LUISA: ¿Cuántas lenguas hablas?
    JOHN: Dos, inglés y español. Y ¿tú?
    LUISA: Sólo español.

4 MARÍA: Betty, ¿tienes hermanos?
    BETTY: Una hermana, y ¿tú?
    MARÍA: Dos hermanos.

Exercise 8

Here are some answers. What were the questions?

1 Soy de Vitoria
2 Al hotel María Cristina
3 Tres, inglés, alemán y español
4 Bien, gracias

5 No tiene fax pero sí teléfono
6 Sí y ésta también

Exercise 9

How would you ask for rooms in the following situations?

1 You are with a friend
2 You are with your husband/wife
3 You are with your partner and two children
4 You are with two friends. You would like to share one room
5 You are on your own
6 You need five single rooms for a group

Exercise 10

Rewrite the dialogue between Michael and the receptionist but this time Michael wants a double room for two nights. (Note **doble** double.)

Exercise 11

Here is a series of conjugated verbs. Fill in the gaps:

tener	**viajar**	**llevar**	**venir**
tengo	_____	_____	vengo
_____	viajas	_____	_____
tiene	_____	lleva	_____
ser	**cobrar**	**trabajar**	**recibir**
_____	cobro	_____	_____
eres	_____	trabajas	recibes
_____	cobra	_____	_____

Exercise 12

Fill in the gaps with the appropriate verb for the different contexts.
The verbs are: **vivir**, **estar**, **ser**, **hablar**, **trabajar** (to work), **viajar** (to travel) and **comer** (to eat).

1 Normalmente _____ en restaurantes italianos. (Yo)
2 ¿_____ con tus padres? (Tú)
3 _____ muy cansado porque _____ mucho. (Él)

4 _____ de Galicia pero _____ en Santander. (Yo)
5 Sólo _____ un poco de español. (Ella)
6 ¿_____ mucho a España? (Tú)

Exercise 13

You want to know the cost of a few items that you would like to buy. Point to the items and ask for the price.

el plato

la taza

el cenicero

el cuadro

la muñeca

e.g. ¿Cuánto cuesta ese libro?

Vocabulary building

Exercise 14

Match the following numbers:

1	veintidós	(a)	67
2	cuarenta y cuatro	(b)	91
3	sesenta y siete	(c)	58
4	ochenta y nueve	(d)	22
5	treinta y seis	(e)	75
6	cincuenta y ocho	(f)	44
7	noventa y uno	(g)	36
8	setenta y cinco	(h)	89

Exercise 15

The following words have something to do with words you have learnt in this lesson. See if you can match them with their English equivalents.

1	**(el) viaje**	(a)	the call
2	**(el) trabajo**	(b)	long live
3	**(la) llamada**	(c)	the food
4	**viva**	(d)	the job
5	**(la) comida**	(e)	the journey
6	**querido**	(f)	bath
7	**(la) bañera**	(g)	dear

Reading

John is in a hotel asking for a room. (Note **la cama** bed.)

1 How many nights does he want the room for?
2 How many rooms and what sort?

JOHN: Buenas noches, ¿tiene usted dos habitaciones para cuatro noches por favor?

RECEPCIONISTA: ¿Dos habitaciones dobles?

JOHN: No, una doble y una individual.

RECEPCIONISTA: Lo siento señor pero sólo hay habitaciones dobles. Si quiere se puede poner otra cama en la habitación doble.

JOHN: Estupendo, muchas gracias.

4 Direcciones

Directions

In this lesson we will look at:

- asking for directions
- commands
- the verbs **saber**, **conocer**, **haber** and **poder**
- colours
- some more numbers

Dialogue 🔲

Sightseeing in Barcelona

Michael, an Irish tourist in Barcelona, is walking in Las Ramblas, a famous street lined with shops, restaurants, cafés and flower stalls, bird sellers, and kiosks, when he starts to get a headache. He asks two passers-by if there is a chemist's near by

MICHAEL: Oiga, perdone señora, ¿sabe si hay una farmacia cerca de aquí?

SEÑORA: Lo siento señor, pero no soy de aquí.

MICHAEL: No importa, gracias.

MICHAEL: Oiga, perdone señor, ¿sabe si hay una farmacia cerca de aquí?

SEÑOR: ¡Sí claro! Mire, hay una al final de Las Ramblas. Siga todo recto, al final de Las Ramblas gire a la izquierda; la farmacia está a la derecha, al lado de una librería.

MICHAEL: Todo recto, a la izquierda y la farmacia está a la derecha, ¿no?

SEÑOR: Correcto, a unos tres minutos.

MICHAEL: Muchas gracias, señor.

SEÑOR: De nada, joven.

MICHAEL: *Excuse me, madam, do you know if there is a chemist's near by?*

SEÑORA: *I am sorry, sir, but I am not from here.*

MICHAEL: *It does not matter, thank you.*

MICHAEL: *Excuse me, sir, do you know if there is a chemist's near by?*

SEÑOR: *Of course! Look, there is one at the end of Las Ramblas. Carry straight on, at the end of Las Ramblas turn left, the chemist's is on the right, next to a bookshop.*

MICHAEL: *Straight on, turn left and the chemist's is on the right, correct?*

SEÑOR: *Correct, about three minutes away.*

MICHAEL: *Thank you very much, sir.*

SEÑOR: *Not at all, young man.*

Vocabulary

oiga	a formal expression to attract someone's attention	**siga todo recto**	carry straight on (formal)
perdone	excuse me (formal)	**gire**	turn (formal)
sabe	you know (formal)	**a la izquierda**	to the left
si	if	**a la derecha**	to the right
(la) farmacia	chemist's	**al lado de**	next to
cerca de	near	**(la) librería**	bookshop
lo siento	I'm sorry	**correcto**	correct
no importa	It does not matter	**a unos tres minutos**	about three minutes away
mire	look (formal)	**de nada**	not at all, you're welcome
al final	at the end	**(el) joven**	young man/youth

Language in use

Saber *(to know)*

This verb is slightly irregular. The first person singular is the only one that does not follow the rule.

No *sé* dónde está	*I* don't *know* where it is
¿*Sabes* dónde está Lourdes?	Do *you know* where Lourdes is?
Marta no *sabe* la verdad	Marta *doesn*'t *know* the truth
¿*Sabe* si hay un estanco cerca?	Do *you know* if there is a tobacconist's nearby?

There are two verbs in Spanish that can be translated as 'to know': **saber** and **conocer**. When you are talking about places and people, you should use the verb **conocer**.

No *conozco* Marbella	*I* don't *know* Marbella
¿*Conoces* a Pedro?	Do *you know* Pedro?
María no *conoce* a Rosa	María *doesn*'t *know* Rosa

Note that you need to use the preposition **a** after the verb **conocer** when talking about people.

Hay (there is *and* there are)

We use this form to express the existence of people or things.

Hay una habitación libre	*There is* one free room
¿*Hay* mucha gente en tu casa?	*Are there* many people in your house?
¿*Hay* entradas para la película?	*Are there* tickets for the film?

Note that the form **hay** does not change, regardless of the number of things or people it refers to. The same form is used for both singular and plural sentences.

Hay una habitación	*There is* one room
Hay habitaciones	*There are* rooms

If you do not know whether there is a chemist's or a bank, etc., you should use the indefinite article (**un, una**).

¿Hay *una* panadería cerca de aquí?	Is there *a* baker's near by?
¿Hay *una* agencia de viajes en esta calle?	Is there *a* travel agency in this street?

However, when you are asking about somewhere specific, like the British Embassy, you should use the definite article (**el, la**), together with the verb **estar**.

¿Dónde está la embajada británica, por favor?	Where is the British Embassy, please?

Direcciones *(directions)*

a la derecha	to the right
a la izquierda	to the left
todo recto	straight on
al final	at the end
al final de la calle	at the end of the street
la primera calle a la derecha	the first street on the right
la segunda calle a la izquierda	the second street on the left
gire a la izquierda	turn to the left (formal)
coja la primera calle a la derecha	take the first (street) on the right (formal)
coja la segunda a la izquierda	take the second on the left

Imperativo *(commands)*

To make a command, simply use the third person singular of the verb. This applies as long as you are using the informal way of addressing people. Use this form for most verbs, although there are some irregularities.

Habla **más alto por favor**	*Speak* louder, please
Trabaja **menos**	*Work* less
Lleva **estos documentos al jefe**	*Take* these documents to the boss

When you are using the more formal way of addressing people, a different form of the verb is used. For the time being, just learn those that are needed for directions.

Coja **la primera a la derecha**	*Take* the first on the right
Vaya **todo recto**	*Go* straight on
Cruce **la plaza**	*Cross* the square

Ordinal numbers

These numbers take the gender and number of the object they refer to.

Coja la *primera* **calle**	Take the *first* street
Vive en el *segundo* **piso**	S/he lives on the *second* floor
Las *primeras* **casas son modernas**	The *first* houses are modern
Ésta es la *primera* **vez**	This is the *first* time

Note that the word **primero** loses its final **o** when it goes in front of a noun.

    Vive en el *primer* piso   S/he lives on the *first* floor

---

Spanish culture

Señor y señora
You can use the terms **señor** and **señora** when you want to address someone whose name you do not know. This is especially the case if the person is not young. If a woman is young then you should use the term **señorita**. However, the masculine form **señorito** is only used by servants to their young masters! The abbreviated form of **señor** is **Sr.**, of **señora**, **Sra.**, and of **señorita**, **Srta**.

Language in use

Exercise 1

Look at the map and say which of the following instructions are correct if you want to go to a bookshop (**una librería**).

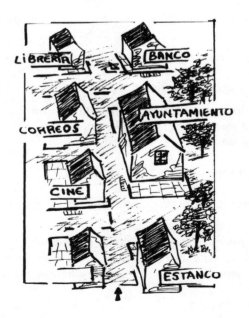

(a) Vas todo recto, coges la primera calle a la derecha, luego la primera a la izquierda y la librería está a la izquierda
(b) Vas todo recto, coges la primera calle a la izquierda, luego la segunda a la derecha y la librería está ahí mismo
(c) Vas todo recto, coges la tercera calle a la izquierda y la librería está a la derecha

Exercise 2

Look at the map of Pamplona below. You are in La Plaza del Castillo when someone asks you how to get to La Plaza de Toros (7). Give him/her the right directions.

Exercise 3

The person you are staying with wants you to go to the library to return a book. She has left a note explaining how to get there. (Note **la puerta** the door.)

En la puerta, gira a la derecha, coge la tercera calle a la izquierda, calle San Miguel, cruza la plaza y la biblioteca está en la misma calle a la derecha. ¡Suerte!

Translate the note before you leave the house to make sure you understand.

Exercise 4

It is your first day in Bilbao. You need to go to a few places: the railway station (**la estación**), the tourist office (**la oficina de turismo**), a bookshop (**la librería**), a supermarket (**el supermercado**), a bank (**el banco**) and the Australian embassy. Ask how to get there.

    e.g.   ¿Dónde está la embajada irlandesa?
            ¿Hay una panadería cerca de aquí?

Exercise 5

Write down how to get from your home to the local chemist and the local library (**la biblioteca**).

Dialogue

In the metro

Michael is in Sants station, the main railway station in Barcelona. He asks how to get to the Picasso Museum

MICHAEL: Perdone señor, quisiera ir al Museo de Picasso. ¿Sabe si se puede ir en metro?

SEÑOR: Sí, puede ir a la estación Jaume I y desde allí está a unos cinco minutos andando.

MICHAEL: ¿Qué línea es?

SEÑOR: Mire, no es directo, tiene que cambiar. Coja la línea quinta, dirección a Horta, baje en la estación Verdaguer, creo que es la cuarta parada, y de allí coja la cuarta, dirección a Pep Ventura.

MICHAEL: Vale, muchas gracias.

SEÑOR: De nada.

MICHAEL: *Excuse me sir, I would like to go to the Picasso Museum. Do you know if it is possible to go on the underground?*

SEÑOR: *Yes, you have to go to Jaume I station, and from there is about five minutes' walk.*

MICHAEL: *Which line is it?*

SEÑOR: *It is not direct, you have to change. Take Line V in the direction of Horta. Get off at the Verdaguer station, I think it is the fourth stop, and from there take Line IV in the direction of Pep Ventura.*
MICHAEL: *OK, thanks a lot.*
SEÑOR: *Not at all.*

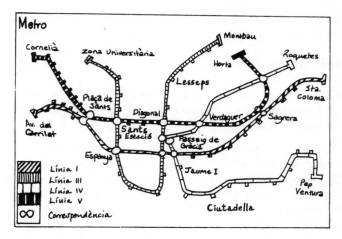

NB: The names on this map are in Catalan, one of the official languages of Catalonia

Vocabulary

quisiera	I would like	**cambiar**	to change
(el) museo	museum	**azul**	blue
se puede	one can	**amarilla**	yellow (feminine)
(el) metro	underground	**(la) dirección**	direction
desde	from	**baje**	get off (formal)
allí	there	**creo que**	I believe that
andando	walk (literally 'walking')	**(la) parada**	stop
(la) línea	line		

Language in use

Quisiera

This is the polite form for asking for things.

Quisiera una habitación	I would like a room

It is also used for expressing an intention to do something.

Quisiera estudiar español	I would like to study Spanish
Quisiera ir al cine	I would like to go the cinema

Poder (*to be able, can*)

Poder is another slightly irregular verb. The 'o' becomes 'ue' in some forms of the verb. This verb is always followed by an infinitive (e.g. **comer**, **ir**, **trabajar**).

No *puedo* comer más	*I cannot* eat any more.
¿Puedes ir a la tienda?	*Can you* go to the shop?
Pedro *puede* venir	Pedro *can* come.
¿Puedo hacer una llamada?	*Can I* make a phone call?
¿Puedes venir esta noche?	*Can you* come tonight?
No *puede* ver bien	*S/he cannot* see well.

You must be careful not to use this verb when you talk about things that have been learned, rather than things that you are physically able to do. For example, to express 'Can you speak Spanish?' Spanish uses the verb **saber**.

¿Sabes nadar?	*Can* you swim?
¿Sabes leer español?	*Can* you read Spanish?
¿Sabes tocar el piano?	*Can* you play the piano?
No *puede* leer porque no ve bien	S/he *cannot* read because s/he cannot see well

Los colores

As they are adjectives, most colours in Spanish will change gender according to the noun they qualify.

La línea *amarilla*	The *yellow* line
El coche *amarillo*	The *yellow* car
La línea *roja*	The *red* line
El autobús *rojo*	The *red* bus

However, the adjectives that end in a consonant or in the vowel 'e' do not change their gender.

La línea *azul*	The *blue* line
El coche *azul*	The *blue* car

There are, in addition, some colours that end in **-a** that do not change gender because of their association with the objects they represent.

Tiene un jersey *rosa*	S/he has a *pink* sweater
Tiene el pelo *naranja*	S/he has *red* (lit. orange) hair
Me gusta el color *lila*	I like the colour *lilac*

Vocabulary

negro	black	**marrón**	brown*
blanco	white	**gris**	grey*
oscuro	dark	**claro**	light

* Note that these do not change gender.

Creer que (*to believe/think that*)

When you are not absolutely certain about something, you can use **creer que**.

Creo que **está en casa**	*I think* s/he is at home
¿*Crees que* **viene hoy?**	*Do you think* s/he is coming today?
Luis *cree que* **va a llamar hoy**	Luis *thinks that* s/he is going to call today

And these expressions are very useful:

Creo que sí	I think so
Creo que no	I do not think so

Pronunciation 🔲

r/rr

The single **r** is rolled when it is at the beginning of a word.

rosa   **rota**
La rosa está rota

It is also rolled when it is placed after the consonants **b, n**, **s** or **l**.

Enrique   **alrededor**   **Israel**
Enrique vive en Israel, en los alrededores de Jerusalén

Double **r** (**rr**) is also pronounced strongly. Double **r** (**rr**) can only go between vowels.

perro   **corre**   **tierra**
El perro corre y tira tierra

If you have the cassettes, listen for the difference between:

perro and **pero**
El perro corre pero está enfermo

Más números

100	cien	230	doscientos/as treinta
101	ciento uno/a	340	trescientos/as cuarenta
102	ciento dos	480	cuatrocientos/as ochenta
103	ciento tres	500	quinient**os**/as
110	ciento diez	520	quinient**os**/as veinte
120	ciento veinte	690	seiscient**os**/as noventa
130	ciento treinta	740	setecient**os**/as cuarenta
170	ciento setenta	860	ochocient**os**/as sesenta
190	ciento noventa	950	novecient**os**/as cincuenta
200	doscientos/as	1000	mil

Note that the number **cien** becomes **ciento** over one hundred. The numbers **doscientos/as**, **trescientos/as**, etc., take the gender of the object they relate to.

Doscientos gramos de jamón   Two hundred grams of ham
Doscientas cajas   Two hundred boxes

It would be useful for you to become used to using the masculine form because **euros**, the Spanish currency, are masculine.

Quinientos euros   Five hundred euros

Pesos, the currency in many Latin American countries, are also masculine.

Cuatrocientos pesos   Four hundred pesos

Dólares (dollars) are also masculine in Spanish:

Trescientos dólares americanos	300 American dollars
Seiscientos dólares australianos	600 Australian dollars

Language in use

Exercise 6

Match the questions with their answers:

1 ¿Puedes ir a ver a Juan?   (a) No, no sabe
2 ¿Sabes nadar bien?   (b) Lo siento, no puedo ir hoy
3 ¿Puedes trabajar un poco   (c) Sí, claro
  más hoy?
4 ¿Sabe Felipe jugar al fútbol? (d) No sé
5 ¿Puedes llevar este libro a   (e) Sé nadar pero no muy bien
  la oficina?
6 ¿Sabes jugar al baloncesto? (f) Sí, luego

Exercise 7

Fill in the gaps with the appropriate verb: **saber**, **conocer** or **poder**:

1 ¿_____ escribir árabe? (tú)
2 ¿_____ venir a casa hoy? (tú)
3 No _____ Francia. (yo)
4 No_____ tocar la guittara. (yo)
5 No_____ hablar francés. (él)
6 ¿ _____ a Pedro. (tú)
7 No _____ ir hoy. (ella)
8 Sí _____ tocar el clarinete. (yo)
9 No _____ jugar al tenis. (él)
10 Ella no _____ a mi hermano.

Exercise 8

Look at the map of Barcelona's underground (see page 49) and answer these questions. (Note: You are at Diagonal.)

1 ¿Para ir a la Zona Universitària tengo que cambiar de línea?
2 ¿Para ir a la estación Sants qué línea es?

3 ¿Para ir al Museo de Picasso qué línea es?
4 ¿Para ir al Passeig de Gràcia tengo que coger la línea quinta?

Exercise 9

You are at Sants Estació where some people ask you how to get to the following stations:
   Lesseps, Jaume I and Ciutadella. Write down the answers.

Exercise 10

Write down five things you would like to do in the future.

   e.g. Quisiera ir a París

Vocabulary building

Exercise 11

Here is a list of things you may want to ask when you are living in a friend's house. There are two slightly odd statements. Can you find them?
   ¿Puedo llamar por teléfono a mi madre?
   ¿Puedo cocinar?
   ¿Puedo ir al cine?
   ¿Puedo usar el ordenador?
   ¿Puedo escribir a mi hermano?
   ¿Puedo ver la televisión por la tarde?

Exercise 12

Here is a list of verbs in the imperative form. Can you match them with their respective contexts? Look for the words you do not know in the glossary.

1 entra	(a) la calle	
2 trabaja	(b) este documento	
3 mira	(c) las escaleras	
4 firma	(d) más	
5 sube	(e) en casa	
6 baja	(f) la televisión	
7 cruza	(g) la radio	

Exercise 13

A friend of yours, who is travelling in South America, needs to know what the exchange rate is in dollars for the peso chileno, the bolivar venezolano and the real brasileño. Look at the exchange rates and write down the information for her.

e.g. **Un dólar vale veintiocho rublos**

CAMBIOS DE MONEDAS EN DÓLARES EST ADOUNIDENSES	
Nuevo sol peruano	3
Rublo ruso	28
Peso chileno	587
Dirham marroquí	4
Bolivar venezolano	699
Peso mexicano	10
Real brasileño	2
Peso filipino	51
Baht tailandia	43

5 Viajando

Travelling around

In this lesson we will look at:

- asking about departures and arrivals
- talking about the time and the days of the week
- expressing obligation
- the verb **irse**

Dialogue 🔲

At the station

Virginia, a Spanish student, is in Bilbao and wants to go to Burgos to see the cathedral and to stay for a few days. She goes to the station to buy a ticket

VIRGINIA: ¿A qué hora sale el Talgo para Burgos?
EMPLEADO: A las ocho de la mañana todos los días.
VIRGINIA: Bien, un billete para mañana, por favor.
EMPLEADO: ¿De ida y vuelta o ida sólo?
VIRGINIA: De ida sólo, no sé cuando voy a volver, martes o miércoles.
EMPLEADO: Está bien, un billete de ida. Son 20 euros.
VIRGINIA: Bien, aquí tiene. Muchas gracias. ¡Ah! perdone, ¿de qué vía sale?
EMPLEADO: De la vía 2, andén 1.

VIRGINIA: *What time does the Talgo for Burgos leave?*
EMPLEADO: *At eight a.m. every day.*
VIRGINIA: *OK. A ticket for tomorrow, please.*
EMPLEADO: *A return or a single?*

VIRGINIA: *A single, I don't know when I'm coming back, Tuesday or Wednesday.*
EMPLEADO: *OK. A single ticket. It is twenty euros.*
VIRGINIA: *Here you are. Oh! Excuse me, which platform does it leave from?*
EMPLEADO: *From line 2, platform 1*

Vocabulary

(la) hora	time (literally, hour)
sale	it leaves
Talgo	the name of a type of fast train
todos	all (masculine)
(el) billete	ticket (for travel)
ida y vuelta	return (ticket)
ida sólo	one way
cuando	when
volver	to return
(la) vía	line
(el) andén	platform

¿A qué hora? *(At what time?)*

¿A qué hora vienes?	(At) what time are you coming?
A las doce	At twelve o'clock.
¿A qué hora abren los bancos?	What time do the banks open?
A las nueve de la mañana	At nine o'clock in the morning
¿A qué hora empieza la obra?	What time does the play start?
A las ocho	At eight o'clock
¿A qué hora sale el avión?	What time does the plane leave?
A la una	At one o'clock
¿A qué hora es la reunión?	What time is the meeting?
A las diez de la mañana	At 10 a.m.

You will probably have noticed that the article **la** is always plural except for 'one o'clock'

a las doce	at twelve o'clock
a la una	at one o'clock

When you want to specify a.m. or p.m. use **de la mañana**, **de la tarde** or **de la noche**.

¿A qué hora es la reunión?	What time is the meeting?
A las ocho de la mañana	At eight a.m.
¿A qué hora es la película?	What time is the film on?
A las once de la noche	At eleven p.m.

Railway and airport timetables use the 24-hour clock.

¿A qué hora sale el avión para Londres?	What time does the plane for London leave?
A las dieciocho horas	At six p.m.

¿Qué hora es?

Son las dos y diez	It's ten past two
Son las tres y veinte	It's twenty past three
Son las cuatro menos cinco	It's five to four
Son las seis menos veinte	It's twenty to six
Son las siete y media	It's half past seven
Es la una y cuarto	It's a quarter past one

Note that to express the time Spanish starts with the hour followed by the minutes.

Días de la semana (days of the week)

El *lunes* voy a estar en casa	I am going to be at home on *Monday*
El *martes* voy a la oficina	I am going to the office on *Tuesday*
El *miércoles* voy a Londres	I am going to London on *Wednesday*
¿Vas el *jueves* a Granada?	Are you going to Granada on *Thursday*?
El *viernes* sale para Madrid	S/he is leaving for Madrid on *Friday*
No viene el *sábado*	S/he is not coming on *Saturday*
¿Viene el *domingo*?	Is s/he coming on *Sunday*?

Note that:

- the days of the week do not have capital letters as they do in English

- when you want to talk about something that happens every Monday, Tuesday, etc., you use the plural form of the noun:

Los *lunes* no voy a la oficina   I don't go to the office on *Mondays*

Los *sábados* estudio alemán   I study German on *Saturdays*

¿Qué haces los *domingos*?   What do you do on *Sundays*?

Spanish culture

When you want to buy a train ticket you ask for the type of train that you want to travel on. *El Talgo* is the fastest train after *El AVE*, the new fast train that links Madrid with Sevilla. The next fastest train is *El TER*. The *Expreso* is slower than the *Talgo* but it is much cheaper. *El Correos* is very slow because, as its name implies, it is the mail train and it stops everywhere. However, it is very cheap and it means you can travel overnight. *El Tranvía* is used for short journeys.

Renfe, the Spanish rail company, offers discounts on journeys taken during *días azules* ('blue days'). These are most of the year with the exception of peak holiday weekends. They offer, amongst other things, 25% discount on return journeys, 50% discount for people over 65 and for children between the ages of 7 and 14 who travel with their family, and up to 25% discount for groups of 10 people or more.

Language in use

Exercise 1

It is your second day in Spain and you need the opening times of various establishments (banks, museums, supermarkets, restaurants, chemists and the post office (*correos*)). You go to the tourist office to ask someone.

> e.g. ¿A qué hora abren las farmacias?
>   ¿A qué hora cierran las farmacias?

Exercise 2

Study the timetable at the railway station and answer the following questions:

1 ¿A qué hora sale el tren para Burgos?
2 ¿A qué hora sale el tren para Valencia?
3 ¿Hay trenes para Barcelona?
4 ¿Sale el tren para Toledo antes de las cuatro?
5 ¿A qué hora llega el tren de Bilbao?
6 ¿A qué hora llega El AVE de Sevilla?

HORARIO DE LLEGADA Y SALIDA DE TRENES
SALIDAS

Tren	Destino	Hora	Vía
Talgo	Burgos	15.30	3
Tranvía	Toledo	16.15	1
TER	Valencia	17.45	2
Talgo	Gerona	18.30	4

LLEGADAS

Tren	Procedencia	Hora	Vía
Talgo	Alicante	16.40	5
AVE	Sevilla	18.30	2
Expreso	Miranda	19.15	3
Talgo	Bilbao	21.00	2

Exercise 3

You are buying tickets for yourself and for a group of students who do not speak Spanish. One wants a return ticket to Valencia, another one wants to go to Granada but does not know when she is returning, another wants to go to Cuenca and return on Sunday, and you want to visit a friend in Zaragoza. Write four short dialogues.

Exercise 4

Your boss wants to know what her employees do in the evening because she is thinking of running some language courses. She has asked you to write down what you do on the different days of the week.

Exercise 5

Match the following times:

1	Son las once menos diez	(a)	12.15
2	Son las cuatro y veinte	(b)	8.05
3	Son las siete y media	(c)	10.50
4	Son las doce y cuarto	(d)	12.35
5	Es la una menos veinticinco	(e)	4.20
6	Son las ocho y cinco	(f)	19.30

Exercise 6

There is an Almodóvar film season. If you have the cassettes, listen and then tell your friend at what time the following films start:

Qué he hecho para merecer ésto .
La ley del deseo
Mujeres al borde de un ataque de nervios
Tacones lejanos

Dialogue

Talking about plans

Virginia is about to take the train to Burgos when she bumps into a friend

SARA: Virginia, ¿qué haces por aquí?
VIRGINIA: Me voy a pasar unos días a Burgos.
SARA: ¡Ah, estupendo! ¿Vas a estar allí mucho tiempo?
VIRGINIA: Sólo unos días, tengo que volver antes del día ocho ya que tengo una entrevista en la empresa 'CASAS'. Mira, perdona Sara, tengo que irme, el tren sale en cinco minutos.

SARA: Tranquila, buena suerte en la entrevista y que te lo pases bien en Burgos.
VIRGINIA: Gracias, hasta pronto.

SARA: *Virginia, what are you doing here?*
VIRGINIA: *I am going to spend a few days in Burgos.*
SARA: *Brilliant! Are you going to stay long?*
VIRGINIA: *Only a few days. I have to come back before the eighth as I have an interview with the firm 'CASAS'. Look, excuse me Sara but I have to go. The train leaves in five minutes.*
SARA: *Don't worry! Good luck with the interview and have a good time in Burgos.*
VIRGINIA: *Thank you, see you soon.*

Vocabulary

haces	you do
me voy	I am going
pasar	to spend (time)
estupendo	brilliant
semana	week
tengo que	I have to
antes de	before
ya que	since
(la) entrevista	the interview
(la) empresa	the firm
tranquila(o)	An expression meaning 'don't worry'
buena suerte	good luck
que te lo pases bien	have a good time

Language points

Irse *and reflexive verbs*

The verb **ir**, when used reflexively (i.e. when the action of the verb is performed on the subject, e.g. 'he washed himself'), takes the meaning of 'to be about to leave' or 'to go away'. This type of verb takes the following reflexive pronouns: **me**, **te**, **se**

Me voy a Londres	I am going to London
¿Te vas de vacaciones?	Are you going on holiday?

Se va al extranjero	S/he is going abroad
Se va del trabajo	S/he is leaving the job

To use reflexive verbs in the formal way, you have to take the third person of the verb and the third person reflexive pronoun as well.

¿Se va usted ahora?	Are you (formal) leaving now?

Notice that reflexive pronouns normally go in front of the verb. However, when there are two verbs, one of which is in the infinitive, the pronoun can go in front of the first verb or after the infinitive. When this is the case the pronoun joins the infinitive.

Tengo que irme	I have to leave
Me tengo que ir	I have to leave
¿Te tienes que ir ahora?	Do you have to go now?
Tienes que irte ahora?	Do you have to go now?

Tener que . . . *(to have to . . .)*

In order to express having to do something you can use the verb **tener** plus **que**.

Tengo que terminar esta carta	I have to finish this letter
Tienes que ir al consulado	You have to go to the consulate
Jaime tiene que escribir más	Jaime has to write more
¿Qué tienes que hacer?	What do you have to do?

Antes de/después de

To express the idea of 'before' or 'after' something happens, the following are used:

Después de **ver la película**	*After* seeing the film
Tengo que hacerlo *antes de* **irme**	I have to do it *before* leaving

Note that they take the infinitive (**comer, ver, ir**).

When **antes de** is followed by a masculine noun the preposition **de** joins **el** to become **del**. (Note **el día** day.)

Tengo que volver antes *del* **día 4**	I have to come back before *the* 4th

Pasarlo bien/mal *(to have a good/bad time)*

In order to express 'to have a good/bad time' you need to use the verb **pasar** with or without the reflexive pronouns (**me**, **te**, **se**) and the article **lo**:

Siempre *me lo paso bien* en España	I always *have a good time* in Spain
***¿Te lo pasas bien* aquí?**	*Do you have a good time* here?
Pedro *lo pasa* muy *mal* allí	Pedro *is having a bad time* there

Por

There are two prepositions in Spanish that mean 'for'. These are **por** and **para**. You will see some of the uses of the preposition **para** in lessons 9 and 14. Here are some of the uses of **por**.

You have seen **por aquí** in the dialogue. **Por** is used to express an indefinite place or time:

Van a venir por enero	They are coming around January
El libro tiene que estar por aquí	The book must be around here

The preposition **por** is also used to express a period of time. It is equivalent to **durante** (during).

Se va a quedar aquí por una semana	S/he will stay here for a week

Por also means 'on behalf of', 'instead of'.

María está enferma así que voy a hacer el trabajo por ella.
María is ill so I am going to do the job instead of her.

Pronunciation 📼

Ce/Ci/Ca/Co/Cu

When **c** goes before an **e** or an **i**, the sound is different from when it goes before the vowels **a**, **o** and **u**. If you have the cassettes, listen to the following:

cincuenta	caro	cero	cuesta	coche

Ese coche es muy caro, cuesta cincuenta millones
¿Cuántos ceros?

Language in use

Exercise 7

The following sentences have been mixed up. Can you put the words in the correct order so that they make sense?

1 Pedro vacaciones se de va
2 Luisa va no se Inglaterra a
3 voy a me Nueva York mañana
4 ¿Dónde a vas tarde esta?

Exercise 8

Fill in the appropriate form of the verb **tener**:

– Mañana _____ que ir al dentista. (tú)
– ¿No _____ que ir a la escuela? (yo)
– No, ¡cuántas veces _____ que decirte que mañana _____ que ir al dentista!
– Pero, mamá _____ que hacer un examen mañana. (yo)

Exercise 9

Now write six things you have to do during the next few days:

e.g. **Mañana tengo que comprar los billetes para Londres**

Exercise 10

Answer the following questions:

1 ¿Qué vas a hacer antes de comer?
2 ¿Qué vas a hacer después de cenar?
3 ¿Adónde vas después de ver la película?
4 ¿Vas a estudiar antes de ver la película?
5 ¿Qué vas a hacer después de la entrevista?
6 ¿Adónde va Sonia después de trabajar?

Vocabulary building

Exercise 11

Here are some words derived from others you have looked at.

Try to match them with their English equivalent.

1	**el pasado**	(a)	a businessman
2	**entrevistar**	(b)	to forgive
3	**empresario**	(c)	the shopping
4	**perdonar**	(d)	worth
5	**(las) compras**	(e)	to interview
6	**valor**	(f)	the past

Exercise 12

Here are some common expressions related to the word **hora**. Try to match them with their English equivalent.

1	**¡a buena hora!**	(a)	timetable
2	**a la hora**	(b)	o'clock
3	**en punto**	(c)	to ask for an appointment
4	**horario**	(d)	congratulations!
5	**¡enhorabuena!**	(e)	punctually
6	**pedir hora**	(f)	about time!
7	**a estas horas**	(g)	now, by now

Reading

Here is some information on the new train that runs between Madrid and Sevilla. Read the information and answer the following questions.

1 How many people can travel on the train?
2 Which factors contribute to the price of the tickets?
3 How long does the journey take?

El AVE, la nueva línea entre Madrid y Sevilla

Seis trenes van a cubrir diariamente el trayecto Madrid–Sevilla con ocho vagones para trescientos veintinueve viajeros. Están distribuidos en tres categorías: club, preferente y turista. Además hay tres tarifas según el horario: valle, punta y llano. El billete Madrid–Sevilla en clase turista a las tres de la tarde – hora valle – cuesta 40 euros. En hora punta, a las siete de la mañana, 55, y en horario llano, a la una de la tarde, 46 euros.

En los vagones, los monitores proyectan durante el viaje un documental de la ciudad de llegada y una película.

El viaje entre Madrid y Sevilla dura 2.50 horas.

Reading

Do you know at what time Spanish meals are eaten? Read the following text and answer the questions.

En España, la gente come normalmente entre la una y las dos, dependiendo del trabajo. Se llama la comida o el almuerzo y es fuerte. En general se cena entre las nueve y las diez. Se llama la cena y es más ligera que la comida. Antes de comer al mediodía, normalmente la gente que trabaja va al bar a tomar una copa y un pincho.

¿A qué hora es el almuerzo en España?
¿A qué hora es la cena en España?

Now answer the following questions.

1 ¿A qué hora comes normalmente?
2 ¿Comes mucho al mediodía?
3 ¿A qué hora cenas normalmente?
4 ¿A qué hora vas a dormir normalmente?
5 ¿A qué hora estudias español?
6 ¿A qué hora sales del trabajo?

6 Comiendo en un restaurante

Eating out

In this lesson we will look at:

- arranging a meeting
- going to a restaurant
- expressing convenience
- the plural forms of the verbs ending in **-ar** and **-er**
- the verbs **quedar** and **acabar**
- more pronouns

Dialogue

Dining out

Susana, an American student, is talking to two Spanish friends about going out to dinner

LUIS: ¿Cenamos esta noche fuera?

SUSANA: ¡Qué buena idea!

PEDRO: Bien, pero tiene que ser un restaurante económico, no tengo mucho dinero.

LUIS: ¿Qué os parece el mesón que acaban de abrir en la Calle Serrano?

PEDRO: ¿Es barato?

LUIS: Sí, creo que sí.

SUSANA: ¿A qué hora quedamos?

PEDRO: A las nueve y media ¿os va bien?

LUIS: A mí sí. ¿Y, a ti Susana?

SUSANA: A mí también.

PEDRO: Vale, a las nueve y media en el bar 'Manolo'.

Language points

Up to now we have been working with the singular form of the verb.

Trabajo en una empresa inglesa	I work in an English firm
¿Cenas en casa esta noche?	Are you eating at home tonight?
Manolo gana mucho dinero	Manolo earns lots of money.

Plural endings

We will now start looking at the plural endings for the verbs ending in **-ar**: **quedar** to arrange to meet (among other meanings).

¿Quedamos en casa de Juan?	Should we meet at Juan's house?
¿Quedáis siempre aquí?	Do you always arrange to meet here?
Quedan siempre en la plaza	They always arrange to meet in the square.

More verbs:

Trabajamos en la embajada	We work in the embassy
¿Dónde trabajáis?	Where do you (plural) work?
Siempre hablan de lo mismo	They always talk about the same things

The personal pronouns are:

nosotros / nosotras	we (masculine and feminine)
vosotros / vosotras	you (plural, masculine and feminine)
ellos / ellas	they (masculine and feminine)
***Nosotros* estamos cansados**	*We* (masculine) are tired
¿Estáis *vosotras* contentas?	Are *you* (plural, feminine) happy?
***Ellos* están nerviosos**	*They* (masculine) are nervous

When the pronoun refers to both men and women, the masculine plural form is used.

You might remember that the verbs **gustar** and **parecer**, etc. are unusual in that they need indirect pronouns.

Me parece bien	*I think* it is OK.
¿Te gusta éste?	*Do you like* this one?
A Pedro no le gusta	Pedro *does not like it*

Here are the plural forms of these pronouns:

Nos **gusta esa casa**	*We* like that house
¿Qué *os* **parece ésa?**	What do *you* (plural) think of that one?
Les **parece bien**	*They* think it is OK.
Nos **gusta salir mucho**	*We* like to go out a lot
¿*Os* **gusta el marisco?**	Do *you* (plural) like shellfish?
Les **parece bien**	*They* think it is OK.

Acabar de

Acabar de is used to express something that has just been done.

Acabo de **hablar con ella**	I *have just* talked to her
¿Acabas de **comer?**	Have *you just* eaten?
Acaba de **salir**	S/he *has just* left
Acabamos de **terminar**	We *have just* finished
¿Acabáis de **llegar?**	Have *you* (plural) *just* arrived?
Acaban de **llamar**	*They have just* called

Ir bien/mal

This is an expression meaning 'to suit'. It needs the verb **ir** plus an indirect object.

Me va **bien a las doce**	Twelve o'clock *suits me*
¿Te va **bien a las tres?**	Does three o'clock *suit you*?
No *le va* **bien hoy**	It does not *suit him/her* today
Me va **mal hoy**	Today does not *suit me*
¿Te va **mejor mañana?**	Does tomorrow *suit you* better?

Prepositional pronouns

Pronouns followed by a preposition are the same as the subject pronouns with the exception of **yo** and **tú** which change to **mí** and **ti**.

A *mí* **me va bien**	It suits *me*
¿A *ti* **te va bien?**	Does it suit *you*?

A *él* le va bien	It suits *him*
A *nosotros* nos va bien	It suits *us*

Note that the pronoun **mí** has an accent and **ti** does not. This is to distinguish it from the possessive adjective **mi**.

Mi coche está afuera	My car is outside

With the preposition **con**, the pronouns **mí** and **ti** form one word:

¿Vienes *conmigo*?	Are you coming *with me*?
¿Va Pedro *contigo*?	Is Pedro going *with you*?

Spanish culture

Spain is a sociable country and Spanish people spend a lot of time in bars and restaurants, or simply out in the streets. Most people do not arrange to meet in their homes; the norm is to arrange to meet in a bar. Bars are often full of families with children. Nowadays there are two distinct kinds of bars: those like **tascas**, **bodegas**, **cervecerías** and **tabernas** where people go to have a drink with **tapas** or **pinchos** (snacks to which you help yourself from the counter and pay later), and night bars, called '**pubs**', frequented by young people in the evening and late at night. These bars look very modern.

If you want to have a full meal you should go to a **comedor** or a **restaurante**.

Comedores are usually attached to a bar. They are cheap places to eat. People who work a long way from home eat a full meal in a *comedor* and settle the bill at the end of the month.

Restaurantes can also be as cheap as **comedores** if you eat the **menú del día**; this is a fixed-priced menu which normally consists of a two-course meal with fruit and wine. Restaurants do not usually offer these menus in the evening when you have to eat **a la carta**.

Language in use

Exercise 1

Match the questions with an appropriate answer:

¡Qué pena!   What a pity!

1 Ese coche cuesta veinte mil euros
2 ¿Te gusta este vestido?
3 Esta casa cuesta doscientos mil euros
4 Marina va a trabajar en la embajada
5 Pedro no puede venir

(a) ¡Qué bonito!
(b) ¡Qué pena!
(c) ¡Qué caro!
(d) ¡Qué cara!
(e) ¡Qué suerte!

Exercise 2

Answer the following questions using the expression **acabar de**.

    e.g.   ¿Cuándo vas a comprar la casa?
            Acabo de comprarla

1 ¿Cuándo va a venir?
2 ¿Cuándo vas a llamarle?
3 ¿Cuándo va a irse?
4 ¿Cuándo vas a terminarlo?
5 ¿Cuándo vas a leer el artículo?
6 ¿Cuándo va a salir?

Exercise 3

You want to arrange to go out to dinner with a group of friends. Phone them and ask if the time you would like to go suits them too.

    e.g.   **Pedro, ¿te va bien a las diez?**
            No, lo siento, me va mejor a las nueve

Exercise 4

Fill in the gaps in the following verb table. Look in the Glossary for the meaning of the verbs you do not know.

andar	*ganar*	*comprar*	*mandar*	*sacar*	*irse*
ando			mando		me voy
	ganas			sacas	
		compra			se va
andamos			mandamos		nos vamos
	ganáis			sacáis	
		compran			se van

Exercise 5

Write a similar dialogue to the first one in this lesson, but this time arrange to go the cinema after meeting up in a local bar.

Dialogue 🔲

En el restaurante

LUIS: ¿Tienen una mesa libre para tres personas, por favor?

CAMARERA: Sí, claro. Hay una mesa libre allí al fondo ¿Les parece bien aquélla?

LUIS: Perfecto, gracias.

Luis, Susana and Pedro sit at the table

PEDRO: ¿Nos trae la carta, por favor?

PEDRO: ¿Qué nos recomienda? ¿Cuál es la especialidad de la casa?

CAMARERA: De pescado les puedo recomendar el rape y el lenguado, y de carnes, hay cordero asado muy bueno.

PEDRO: Bien, gracias. Mientras decidimos ¿puede traernos una botella de vino tinto?

CAMARERA: ¿El vino de la casa?

PEDRO: Sí.

Language points

The endings of *-er* verbs

Como muy poco	*I eat* very little
¿Comes con nosotros?	Will *you eat* with us?

Yolanda sólo com*e* verduras	Yolanda only *eats* vegetables
¿Com*emos* aquí?	Should *we eat* here?
¿Com*éis* carne?	Do *you* (plural) *eat* meat?
No com*en* pescado	*They* do not *eat* fish

Tener

***Tengo* poco dinero**	*I have* little money
¿*Tienes* diez euros?	Do *you* have 10 euros?
Luis *tiene* veinte años	Luis *is* 20 years old
***Tenemos* que ir hoy**	*We have* to go today
***Tenéis* que venir pronto**	*You have* to come soon
¿Cuántas habitaciones *tienen*?	How many rooms do *they have*?

In Lesson 5 we saw that reflexive pronouns can go before the verb or after the infinitive. Direct and indirect pronouns behave the same way. Direct pronouns are so called because they replace nouns that are the direct object of the verb.

> e.g. I want *the book* – I want *it*.

Indirect objects are those objects that get the benefit of the action.

> e.g. I bought a book for *Michael* – I bought a book for *him*

You already know indirect objects as they are the ones you use with the verbs **gustar** and **parecer**.

Spanish direct pronouns differ from the indirect ones in the third person. They are **lo/le/los/les** for masculine things and people, and **la/las** for feminine ones.

Veo a *María* todos los días	I see *María* every day
***La* veo todos los días**	I see *her* every day

These pronouns are used differently in some areas of Spain, so do not be surprised if you hear the 'wrong' pronouns being used; it is simply a matter of dialect.

Traer

¿Te *traigo* un café?	Should *I bring* you a coffee?
¿Me *traes* un té?	Will *you bring* me a tea?
Siempre le *trae* un regalo	*S/he* always *brings* him/her a present

Remember that they can go in different positions with an infinitive.

Puedo hacer*lo* esta noche	I can do *it* tonight
Lo puedo hacer esta noche	I can do *it* tonight
¿Puede traer*nos* la carta?	Can you bring *us* the menu?
¿*Nos* puede traer la carta?	Can you bring *us* the menu?
Puedo recomendar*te* ésta	I can recommend *you* this one
Te puedo recomendar ésta	I can recommend *you* this one

¿Cuál . . . ?

Sometimes it is difficult to know the difference between **qué** and **cuál** as both can be translated by 'what'. There are, however, two structures that always take **cuál** instead of **qué**. These are:

Cuál + ser + noun

¿Cuál es la diferencia?	*What* is the difference?
¿Cuál es su coche?	*Which* one is his car?
¿Cuál es la especialidad?	*What* is the speciality?

Cuál + de + noun

¿Cuál de los dos bolis quieres?	*Which* one of the two pens do you want?
¿Cuál de los tres libros prefieres?	*Which* one of the three books do you prefer?
¿Cuál de las dos camisas te gusta más?	*Which* of the two shirts do you like more?

Pronunciation

Traditional grammar books will tell you that the correct way to pronounce **ll** is as a double 'l', close to the sound of the 'l' in 'battalion'. Many Spanish speakers, however, pronounce it like the Spanish sound **y**, which is quite similar to the English 'j'. This is known as **yeísmo**.

Me llamo Ana
¿Llueve poco en Sevilla?
¿Llevas las llaves?

Language in use

Exercise 6

Choose between **qué** and **cuál**.

1 ¿_____ tienes en la mano?
2 ¿_____ vas a tomar?
3 ¿_____ de los dos prefieres?
4 ¿_____ es tu número de teléfono?
5 ¿_____ comes?
6 ¿_____ estudias?
7 ¿_____ es tu casa?
8 ¿_____ de los dos es tu hermano?

Exercise 7

You have invited a group of friends to your house. One of them wants a coffee, another wants tea, one wants Coke, and another wants an orange juice. Write down their requests.

(el) zumo de naranja   orange juice

   e.g. **¿Me traes un vaso de agua?**

Exercise 8

Answer the following questions using some of the pronouns you have learned.

   e.g.   **¿Dónde compras normalmente *la fruta*?**
         La compro en el supermercado

1 **¿Dónde compras normalmente los jerseis?**
2 **¿Adónde vas a ver normalmente las películas?**
3 **¿Cuándo ves a Juan?**
4 **¿Cuándo llamas normalmente a tu madre?**

Exercise 9

Fill in the gaps in the verb tables:

tener	*leer*	*ver*	*saber*	*vender*
tengo		veo	sé	
	lees	ves		vende
			sabe	
tenemos		vemos		vendemos
	leéis			
tienen		ven		venden

Exercise 10

Write a similar dialogue to the last one, but this time you go to a restaurant with three friends. Ask for a table. The speciality of the house is tuna fish. You want a bottle of white wine instead of red.

Vocabulary building

Exercise 11

Arrange the following food items into four lists: meat, fish, vegetables and fruit:

   verduras   *pescado*   *carne*   *fruta*

merluza, chuletas de cerdo, anchoas, espárragos, naranjas, tomates, sardinas, plátano, coliflor, filete de vaca, atún, judías verdes, pollo, uvas, manzanas

Reading

Read the following article about a new sandwich (**bocadillo**) place that has just opened in Madrid and find the answers to the following questions:

1 **¿Dónde está?**
2 **¿Cuál es la especialidad de la casa?**
3 **¿Cúanto cuestan los bocadillos?**
4 **¿Cúando cierran los jueves y viernes?**

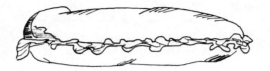

Acaba de nacer un establecimiento madrileño Tomatoma que vende bocadillos calientes y fríos desde primeras horas de la noche hasta casi el amanecer. Hay bocadillos de jamón serrano y queso manchego, atún con pimientos y anchoas con tomate, por ejemplo; o calentitos, de tortilla, o morcilla. La especialidad de la casa es el bocato de lacón con queso, y cuesta lo mismo que el resto de sus hermanos: dos euros.

Abren lunes, martes y miércoles hasta las tres de la madrugada, y el resto de los días, hasta las seis. Los domingos cierran.

7 Una visita al médico

A visit to the doctor

In this lesson we will look at:

- Asking why
- talking about 'how long'
- expressing possession
- simple conditional sentences
- more imperatives
- the verbs **doler**, **encontrarse** and **quedarse**

Dialogue

Going to the doctor's

Sara goes to visit Vicky, an English friend of hers. She finds her in bed feeling unwell

SARA: Hola Vicky. ¿Qué tal estás? Hace mucho que no te veo.

VICKY: Pues no muy bien. Desde hace dos días tengo un dolor de cabeza increíble.

SARA: ¿Has ido al médico?

VICKY: No.

SARA: ¿Por qué no?

VICKY: Es que odio las consultas de médicos. Además como sólo llevo aquí dos meses, no tengo médico de cabecera.

SARA: Pero mujer, si vas al médico puedes tomar algo y ponerte bien rápido. ¿Por qué no vas a mi médico?

VICKY: Vale, pero ¿te importa venir conmigo?

SARA: No, claro que no. ¿Vamos esta tarde?

VICKY: De acuerdo. ¿Te importa llamar tú por teléfono para pedir hora?

SARA: No, llamo ahora.

Language in use

The conditional *si*

The conjunction (a word that joins words, phrases or sentences) **si** is the most usual link word used to express a condition. Although it can be followed by different tenses, at the moment we will only look at those sentences that take **si** with the present tense. When the word **si** is followed by a present tense then the other verbs can go in the present, future or imperative form.

Si vienes te invito a comer	If you come I ask you to have lunch
Si vienes, llámame	If you come, call me
Si vas ahora puedes hablar con él	If you go now you can talk to him
Si lo haces pronto llámame	If you do it soon, call me

Do not mistake the conjunction **si** (without an accent) for the adverb **sí** (with an accent).

¿Por qué . . . ?

When you want to ask 'why' you should use **por qué**. When you want to respond you can use the same words put together as one word and without an accent.

¿Por qué **no vas al médico?**	*Why* don't you go to the doctor?
Porque **tengo miedo**	*Because* I am frightened
¿Por qué **no vas a clase hoy?**	*Why* don't you go to the class today?
Porque **tengo dolor de cabeza**	*Because* I have a headache

In an informal situation, you may hear the word **por** on its own, meaning **por qué**.

No voy a la fiesta	I am not going to the party
¿Por . . . ?	Why?

In addition, you can use the expression **es que** to introduce an excuse or to justify something.

¿Por qué no vas al médico?	Why don't you go to the doctor?
Es que **tengo miedo**	*Because* (the fact is) I am frightened

You will also hear the expression **pues** which we looked at in Lesson 2, with the meaning 'why'. This is also colloquial.

No voy a ir al cine	I am not going to the cinema
¿Pues?	Why?

¿Te importa . . . ?

This is another verb that is conjugated like the verbs **gustar** and **parecer**, and therefore it needs an indirect object. It is followed by an infinitive as long as both verbs refer to the same person. It cannot be followed by an infinitive in phrases such as 'Do you mind if I come?' because the verbs 'mind' and 'come' refer to two different people. We will look at this later on in the book.

¿*Te importa* ir con él?	Do *you mind* going with him?
¿*Te importa* venir a las nueve?	Do *you mind* coming at 9?
No *me importa* ir	*I* don't *mind* going
A Pedro no *le importa* ir	*Pedro* does not *mind* going

Possessive adjectives

Possessive adjectives are used to denote possession (e.g. my, your, etc.). The Spanish possessive adjectives **mi**, **tu** and **su** take the number but not the gender of the object that is possessed.

Mi **hermana vive aquí**	*My* sister lives here
Mi **hermano vive aquí**	*My* brother lives here
Mis **hermanos viven aquí**	*My* brothers live here
¿Dónde están *tus* libros?	Where are *your* books?
Su **madre está enferma**	*His/her/their* mother is ill
Sus **padres viven en Londres**	*His/her/their* parents live in London

Although **su** can mean 'his', 'her', 'their', or 'your' (formal), the meaning is usually conveyed by the context. The possessive adjectives **nuestro** (our) and **vuestro** (your) take the number and gender of the object.

Nuestra **casa está vacía**	*Our* house is empty
Nuestros **padres están ahí**	*Our* parents are there

Nuestras **primas viven en Lugo** *Our* cousins (female) live in
Lugo
¿Dónde están *vuestras* bolsas? Where are *your* bags?

Spanish culture

Spain has reciprocal free health agreements with other member
states of the European Union (EU). If you are from a country outside
the EU, you will have to pay for medical services. For minor complaints you can go to a **farmacia** where you can get many drugs which
would be on prescription in other countries. If you need a chemist outside normal hours you can find out which is the **farmacia de guardia**
(the chemists which have to be open outside normal hours, according
to a rota) by looking in the local newspaper.

Language in use

Exercise 1

As you have not been in Spain for long you do not feel too confi-
dent about going to places on your own. Ask a friend of yours if s/he
does not mind going with you to the doctor, to the hospital, to the
airport, to the station, and to a chemist.

e.g. **¿Te importa venir conmigo al cuartel de policía?**

Exercise 2

Match the questions with the answers:

tan pronto so early   **tan tarde** so late

1 ¿Por qué no vas al cine?   (a) Es que no me gusta
                                        llegar tarde

2 ¿Por qué no bebes más?   (b) Porque me gusta mucho
3 ¿Por qué estudias español?   (c) Es que es muy arrogante
4 ¿Por qué vienes tan tarde?   (d) Es que tengo el coche
5 ¿Por qué vas tan pronto?   (e) Es que me duele la
                                        cabeza

6 ¿Por qué no hablas con ella?   (f) Es que hoy no hay
                                        autobuses

Exercise 3

Answer the following questions:

> e.g. ¿Por qué no vas con él?
>   Es que no me gusta

1 ¿Por qué no comes más?
2 ¿Por qué no vas hoy al colegio?
3 ¿Por qué estás aquí?
4 ¿Por qué sales poco?
5 ¿Por qué no vas al hospital?
6 ¿Por qué no vienes conmigo?

Exercise 4

Match the two halves of the following sentences:

1 Si le ves   (a) puedes cenar con nosotros
2 Si te duele mucho   (b) te doy un caramelo
3 Si vas ahora   (c) dile la verdad
4 Si vienes pronto   (d) llámame
5 Si llega mañana   (e) toma una aspirina
6 Si comes todo   (f) llegas a tiempo

Exercise 5

A friend of yours is working as an au pair. Her Spanish is still very weak, so she has asked you to translate a message her employers have left for her.

Susan, estoy en el hospital 'San Lorenzo' porque Pedrito tiene un dolor de cabeza muy fuerte. Si llegas pronto, por favor prepara algo para cenar, creo que hay unas chuletillas de cordero en el congelador. Si no estoy en casa antes de las ocho llama a mi marido a la oficina y dile donde estoy. Gracias.

Exercise 6

You live with a group of Spanish friends. You seem to have mislaid some of your things: your Spanish books, your wallet, your shoes, and your pen. How would you ask for them?

Dialogue 🔲

En la consulta del médico

Vicky is at the doctor's. He examines her, and recommends that she goes to bed

DOCTOR: Buenas tardes, pase y siéntese por favor. Bien, dígame.
VICKY: Mire, me duele muchísimo la cabeza. Creo que tengo fiebre y además me duelen hasta los huesos.
DOCTOR: ¿Desde cuándo se siente así?
VICKY: Desde hace dos días.
DOCTOR: Bien, déjeme examinarla . . . Sí, tiene usted la gripe. No es grave, lo mejor que puede hacer usted es irse a la cama y quedarse allí unos días. Si después de una semana no se encuentra mejor, vuelva.
VICKY: ¿Tengo que tomar algo?
DOCTOR: Sí, le voy a recetar unos antibióticos. ¿Es usted alérgica a la penicilina?
VICKY: No.
DOCTOR: Aquí tiene la receta.
VICKY: Muchas gracias, adiós.

Doler

Doler is another verb that is conjugated like the verb **gustar**. It therefore needs an indirect object. The endings do not change according to the person, but to the thing that is hurting.

Me duele **la cabeza**	*My* head *aches*
¿Te duele **la garganta?**	*Does your* throat *hurt*?
Le duele **el estómago**	*His/her* stomach *aches*
Me duelen **las piernas**	*My* legs *ache*
¿Le duele **el brazo?**	*Does your (formal)* arm *hurt*?

Note that in Spanish we do not use the possesive pronoun (my, your, etc.) when we talk about parts of the body.

Encontrarse

This verb has three main meanings: 'to meet someone (not for the first time)', 'to feel fine' or 'unwell', and 'to be in a place'.

No me encuentro bien	I don't feel well
¿Te encuentras mal?	Do you feel ill?
Se encuentra mejor	S/he feels better
Me encuentro con él todos los días	I meet him every day
Deben de encontrarse ya en Madrid	They must be in Madrid by now

Sentirse bien/mal

This verb means 'to feel'. It is a reflexive verb, and it is irregular. The **e** becomes **ie** with the exception of the first and second person plural, as with the verb **tener**.

Me siento mal	I feel ill
¿Te sientes bien?	Do you feel well?
María se siente mejor	María feels better

Lo mejor/lo peor

The adjective **mejor** can mean both 'better' and 'best'. When you wish to compare two people you need **que**. However, when you want to say someone is the best, you need to use the articles **el** or **la**.

Pedro es *mejor que* Luis	Pedro is *better than* Luis
Pedro es el *mejor*	Pedro is the *best*
Lola es la *mejor*	Lola is the *best*

When you are talking generally, use the neutral form **lo mejor**.

***Lo mejor* que puedes hacer es ...**	*The best thing* you can do is ...

The adjective **peor** ('worse' and 'worst') is used in the same way as **mejor**:

Juan es *peor que* Manolo	Juan is *worse than* Manolo
Carmen es la *peor*	Carmen is the *worst*
Carlos es el *peor*	Carlos is the *worst*
***Lo peor* que puedes hacer es ...**	*The worst thing* you can do is ...

More imperatives

Remember the formal imperatives we learnt in Lesson 4: **coja**, **vaya**, **cruce**? In the earlier dialogue you saw a few more.

Pase y siéntese	Come in and sit down
Dígame	Tell me
Déjeme examinarle	Let me examine you
Tome estos antibióticos	Take these antibiotics
Vuelva mañana	Come back tomorrow

When the verb is an **-ar** regular verb, then the verb takes the ending **e**:

Habl*e* más despacio, por favor	*Speak* more slowly please
Tom*e* estos antibióticos	*Take* these antibiotics

When the verb is an **-er** or an **-ir** regular verb, the verb takes the ending **a**:

Com*a* más, por favor	*Eat* more, please
Sub*a* allí	*Go* up there

However, although there are some irregular verbs that do not follow this rule at all, you can work out most of them if you think of the first person of the present tense.

***Tengo* mi pasaporte aquí**	*I have* my passport here
***Tenga* mi pasaporte**	*Have* my passport
***Vuelvo* mañana**	*I will come* back tomorrow
***Vuelva* mañana**	*Come back* tomorrow

Do not forget that the direct, indirect and reflexive pronouns go after the imperative form, and that they join the verb.

***¿Se sienta* usted aquí?**	*Do you* (formal) sit here?
***Siéntese* aquí**	*Sit* here
***¿Te traigo* un café?**	*Shall I bring you* a coffee?
***Tráigame* un café por favor**	*Bring me* a coffee, please
***Tráigale* un té, por favor**	*Bring him/her* a tea, please
***Llámele* el miércoles**	*Call him* on Wednesday
***Póngala* en la mesa**	*Put it* on the table

Quedarse

In the previous lesson we saw the verb **quedar** with the meaning 'to arrange to meet'. When the verb is reflexive then it means 'to stay'.

Me quedo **siempre en el hotel**   *I* always *stay* in the Cosmos
   'Cosmos'   hotel
¿Dónde *te quedas* **en Londres?** Where do *you stay* in London?
¿*Nos quedamos* **aquí?**   Do *we stay* here?

¿Desde cuándo . . . ?

In order to express 'for how long' you need to use **desde cuándo**.
And the reply will start with **desde . . .**

¿*Desde* **cuándo le duele la**   *How long* have you had the
   cabeza?   headache?
Desde **hace dos días**   *For* two days
¿*Desde* **cuándo estudias**   *How long* have you been studying
   español?   Spanish?
Desde **hace dos meses**   *For* two months

Remember that Spanish uses the present tense when the action has begun in the past but continues into the present. The same principle applies to sentences using the time expression **hace**:

¿Cuánto tiempo hace que   How long have you studied
   estudias español?   Spanish for?
¿Cuánto tiempo hace que   How long have you lived here
   vives aquí?   for?

Pronunciation 📼

You will probably know that the Spanish language has a letter that does not exist in any other language, the letter **ñ** (**eñe**). It sounds similar to the sound 'ni' in 'onion'. Practise the following:

niña	**año**	**caña**	**campaña**
peña	**compañero**	**España**	**español**

Este año voy a estudiar español en España
Mi compañero tiene una niña muy bonita

Language in use

Exercise 7

Fill in the gaps in this table of imperative forms:

	traer	volver	llamar	poner	escribir
Presente (1)	traigo	vuelvo	llamo	pongo .	escribo
Imperativo (informal)		vuelve		pon	
Imperativo (formal)	traiga				

Exercise 8

Answer the following questions:

1 ¿Desde cuándo no fumas?
2 ¿Desde cuándo estudias español?
3 ¿Desde cuándo estás en España?
4 ¿Desde cuándo no comes carne?
5 ¿Desde cuándo no comes pescado?
6 ¿Desde cuándo no ves a tu madre?

Exercise 9

Match the following statements:

bailar to dance   **leer** to read

1 Rosa come mucho   (a) le duele la garganta
2 María usa mucho   (b) le duelen los ojos
  el ordenador
3 Rafael baila mucho   (c) le duelen los dedos
4 Sebas habla mucho   (d) le duele el estómago
5 Rocío lee mucho   (e) le duelen los pies

Exercise 10

You are asking your boss which of the following to do now. He is not in a very good mood so he tells you to do it at a later time. Here are his replies. What were your questions?

  e.g. ¿Lo hago ahora?   No, hágalo después

1 No, venga mañana
2 No, hágalo luego
3 No, tráigalo el viernes
4 No, vuelva mañana
5 No, escríbala esta tarde
6 No, llámele el jueves

Exercise 11

You are thinking of going on holiday to several European cities. Ask a friend, who goes often, where she usually stays.

e.g. ¿Dónde te quedas normalmente en París?

Vocabulary building

Exercise 12

Here is a list of some expressions that use the verbs **quedar** or **quedarse**. Try to match them with their English equivalents.

1	**Quedarse cortado**	(a)	To be left with nothing
2	**Quedarse de piedra**	(b)	Not knowing what to say
3	**Quedarse atrás**	(c)	What is the final decision!
4	**Quedarse sin nada**	(d)	To be thunderstruck
5	**¡En qué quedamos!**	(e)	To stay behind
6	**Quedar bien/mal**	(f)	To make a good/bad impression

Exercise 13

Here are some more parts of the body that can be broken in a fall or an accident. Can you divide them into two distinct areas of the body?

el brazo, la rodilla, la muñeca, el tobillo, la cadera, el fémur, el codo, el cuello, la espalda, las costillas, los dedos, la pierna

Reading

Jamie goes to see the doctor because he is not feeling well. However, there is nothing wrong with him, with the exception of his lifestyle. Read the dialogue and answer the following questions:

1 Where has he got a pain?
2 What exercise does he do?
3 What does the doctor recommend?

MÉDICO: ¿Qué le pasa?
JAMIE: Mire, doctor, que estoy muy malito.
MÉDICO: ¿Qué le duele?
JAMIE: Doler, doler, nada, pero no me encuentro bien.
MÉDICO: Vamos a ver, ¿fuma usted?
JAMIE: Pues sí, doctor.
MÉDICO: ¿Desde cuándo fuma?
JAMIE: Desde hace veinte años.
MÉDICO: ¿Cuántos cigarrillos fuma al día?
JAMIE: Un paquete más o menos.
MÉDICO: Y ¿bebe usted?
JAMIE: Un poco sólo, normalmente bebo vino con las comidas, unas cervezas con los amigos después del trabajo, y una copita después de cenar.
MÉDICO: ¿Hace usted algún deporte?
JAMIE: Deporte, deporte no, pero de vez en cuando voy al monte.
MÉDICO: Mire, señor. Deje de fumar, deje de beber, haga un poco de ejercicio y si todavía no se encuentra bien, vuelva de nuevo.
JAMIE: ¿Eso es todo . . .?
MÉDICO: Bueno, si puede vaya a vivir al campo.

Here is this week's horoscope for your health. Read it and answer the following questions.

1 Which signs will have good health?
2 Which sign will have stomach problems?
3 Which sign will have headaches?

HORÓSCOPO Semana del 25 de febrero al 4 de marzo

ARIES
Salud: Vas a tener mucha vitalidad.

TAURO:
Salud: El punto débil para esta semana es el estómago. Cuida tu alimentación.

GEMINIS
Salud: Muy buena.

CÁNCER
Salud: Necesitas alimentarte bien.

LEO
Salud: Vitalidad variable. Unas veces te vas a sentir lleno de energía, y otras todo lo contrario.

VIRGO
Salud: Bastante buena, en general.

LIBRA
Salud: Tu punto débil va a ser la garganta.

ESCORPIÓN
Salud: Tu punto débil va a ser el aparato respiratorio. No fumes.

SAGITARIO
Salud: Muy buena.

CAPRICORNIO
Salud: Pueden ser frecuentes los dolores de cabeza.

ACUARIO
Salud: Debes controlar los problemas de piel.

PISCIS
Salud: Tu estado físico es excelente. De todas formas procura no cometer excesos con la comida o la bebida.

8 Buscando piso

Flat-hunting

In this lesson we will look at:

- talking about preferences
- different uses of **muy/mucho**
- some adverbs of quantity
- the plural forms of **-ir** verbs
- the verbs **querer** and **funcionar**
- more uses of the verbs **ser** and **estar**

Dialogue

In an estate agency

Mike and Lesley are looking for another flat because they cannot afford to pay the rent where they are living at present. They go to an agency

LESLEY Y MIKE: Buenos días.

EMPLEADO: Buenos días, siéntense por favor. ¿En qué les puedo servir?

LESLEY: Mire, vivimos ahora en un piso en el centro de Madrid, pero queremos mudarnos porque es muy caro y no podemos pagar el alquiler.

EMPLEADO: Bien, ¿dónde les gustaría vivir?

LESLEY: Preferiríamos vivir no muy lejos del centro.

EMPLEADO: Bien. ¿Cuánto pueden pagar al mes?

LESLEY: Como máximo 600 euros.

EMPLEADO: Por este precio saben que no hay pisos grandes. Tiene que ser un apartamento de un dormitorio.

LESLEY: Sí, no importa.

EMPLEADO: Hay uno en la calle Suero de Quiñones. Es muy pequeño pero está recien pintado y es bonito. ¿Quieren ir a verlo?
LESLEY: Sí, claro.

Language points

Vivir

Here are the plural forms of the verbs ending in **-ir**:

Viv*imos* en el centro de Madrid	*We live* in the centre of Madrid
¿Dónde viv*ís*?	Where do *you live*?
Mis padres viv*en* en Burgos	*My parents live* in Burgos
Sal*imos* muy poco	*We go out* very little
¿Qué prefer*ís* beber?	What do *you prefer* to drink?
Dic*en* que Madrid es muy caro	*They say* that Madrid is very expensive

Querer

This verb is irregular. The first **e** becomes **ie** in all forms except **nosotros** and **vosotros**.

Quiero **vivir en el centro**	*I want* to live in the centre
¿Qué *quieres* hacer hoy?	What do *you want* to do today?
El *quiere* ir al cine	He *wants* to go to the cinema
Queremos **estudiar español**	*We want* to study Spanish
¿Qué *queréis* tomar?	What do *you want* to drink?
¿Adónde *quieren* irse?	Where do *they want* to go?

Note that the verb **querer** is followed by an infinitive. Note also that when it is followed by a reflexive verb, the reflexive pronoun joins onto the end of the infinitive or goes before the conjugated form of the verb **querer**.

Me **quiero ir ahora**	I want to leave now
Quiero ir*me* ahora	I want to leave now

Me gustaría

This conditional is formed by adding **ía** to the infinitive. Remember that because we are dealing with the verb **gustar**, this ending does not change according to the different personal forms.

Me gustaría **vivir aquí**   *I would like* to live here
¿Dónde *te gustaría* **vivir?**   Where *would you like* to live?

Debería

This verb is equivalent to the English 'should'. It is used to advise or to suggest something. Note that the verb endings change according to the person referred to.

Deber*ía* **estudiar más**   *I should* study more
Deber*ías* **salir mas**   *You should* go out more
Luis deber*ía* **ir a la universidad**   *Luis should* go to university
Deber*íamos* **salir juntos**   *We should* go out together
Deber*íais* **ir de vacaciones**   *You should* go on holiday
No deber*ían* **fumar**   *They should* not smoke

The conditional can also be used to express what would happen if it were not for some other circumstance:

Iría **pero no puedo**   *I would go* but I cannot
Trabajaría **aquí pero no puede**   *S/he would work* here but s/he cannot

More on *ser* and *estar*

Descriptions

The verb **ser** is used for describing qualities that are considered permanent by the speaker.

La casa *es* **bonita**   The house *is* pretty
Pedro *es* **guapo**   Pedro *is* handsome
Madrid *es* **caro**   Madrid *is* expensive
Manuel *es* **un borracho**   Manuel *is* a drunkard

However, when the quality is not permanent, or it is not considered so by the speaker, the verb **estar** is used.

La casa está muy bonita ahora	The house is very pretty now
Pedro está muy guapo	Pedro looks very handsome
Madrid está muy caro ahora	Madrid is very expensive now
Manuel está borracho	Manuel is drunk

The house has been decorated so now it looks very nice. Pedro looks handsome because of his new hairstyle, his new clothes, etc. Madrid used to be cheaper than it is now. Pedro is drunk today but he is not normally a drunkard.

Muy/mucho

Muy is used with adjectives or with adverbs.

Madrid es *muy* caro	Madrid is *very* expensive
María es *muy* guapa	María is *very* pretty
Esta comida está *muy* buena	This food is *very* good
Esta película está *muy* bien	This film is *very* good

When the description is of a verb then you should use **mucho**.

Esta casa cuesta *mucho*	This house costs *a lot*
Me gusta *mucho* este bar	I like this bar *very much*
Laura trabaja *mucho*	Laura works *a lot*

Spanish culture

Spain has the largest percentage of property owners in the European Union, despite the fact that Spanish banks offer the highest interest rates within the EU. Property prices have risen alarmingly in recent years, and although they have stopped climbing, apartments are still expensive. Madrid is the most expensive place to buy a property, followed by San Sebastián, Barcelona, and Zaragoza. The cheapest properties are found in Teruel and Ciudad Real. If you want to buy a property that is not new, you must go to the Property Registry to find out if it has any duties or mortgages, and to see who the owner is. If you want to sell your property, hire the services of an estate agent. They will charge you 5% of the selling price, but they will help you in the valuation of the property and in dealing with the solicitor.

Language in use

Exercise 1

Match the questions with their respective answers:

1 ¿Quieres hablar con Pedro?   (a)   Preferiría el sábado
2 ¿Quieres ir al cine?   (b)   ¿No tienes La Vanguardia?
3 ¿Quieres estudiar conmigo   (c)   Preferiría hablar con Luis
   mañana?
4 ¿Quieres salir el domingo?   (d)   ¿No te importa si tomo un
                                    té?
5 ¿Quieres un café?   (e)   Vale, ¿aqué sesión?
6 ¿Quieres El País?   (f)   Lo siento, no puedo mañana

Exercise 2

A friend of yours would like to go out with you. However, you do not feel like it so you have to make an excuse. This happens five times, so give five different reasons.

   e.g.   **¿Quieres venir al cine esta noche?**
           Lo siento, me gustaría ir pero me duele la cabeza

Exercise 3

Write down six things you would like to do next year

   e.g. **Me gustaría aprender español**

Exercise 4

Answer the following questions:

(la) carta   letter

1 ¿Dónde viven los reyes de España?
2 ¿A qué hora salís tú y tus amigos normalmente?
3 ¿Recibís muchas cartas en tu casa?
4 ¿Vienes mucho a España?
5 ¿Te escriben mucho tus amigos?

Exercise 5

You are in an estate agent's because you and your partner want to buy an apartment in Spain. Answer the questions the estate agent asks you. (Note: **mudarse** to move house.)

1 ¿En qué zona les gustaría vivir?
2 ¿Cuánto podrían pagar?
3 ¿Les importaría vivir en un décimo piso?
4 ¿Cuántas habitaciones les gustaría tener?
5 ¿Les importaría vivir en las afueras?
6 ¿Cuándo podrían mudarse?

Exercise 6

Read the following description of a famous person and see if you can guess who she is.

Es rubia aunque a veces está morena
Es pequeña
Está muy delgada
Es norteamericana
Es guapa aunque muchas veces está fea
Es cantante y a veces actriz

Exercise 7

Write a description of someone famous.

Dialogue

En el apartamento

Lesley goes to see the apartment without her husband, as he has an appointment elsewhere

EMPLEADO: Es un cuarto piso pero hay ascensor. ¡Oh, no! el ascensor no funciona. Lo siento pero tenemos que subir andando.

LESLEY: No importa, un poco de ejercicio nunca ha hecho daño a nadie.

EMPLEADO: Aquí es. Como ve, el piso es pequeño pero está muy limpio. Además tiene mucha luz.

LESLEY: Sí, las ventanas son muy grandes. ¿Dónde está la cocina?

EMPLEADO: Al fondo, a la izquierda, al lado del comedor.

LESLEY: ¡Ah, sí! Es pequeña pero no está mal. Y el cuarto de baño ¿Dónde está?

EMPLEADO: Allí enfrente. Y el dormitorio está aquí a la derecha.

LESLEY: El cuarto de baño sólo tiene ducha y bidé pero es alegre. Por cierto, ¿hay calefacción central?

EMPLEADO: No, pero hay estufas en todas las habitaciones.

LESLEY: Bien, me gusta bastante pero si no le importa me gustaría hablarlo con mi marido.

EMPLEADO: Sí, claro. Pase por la oficina después.

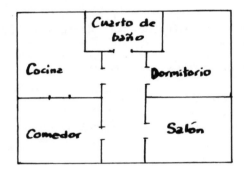

Language points

Funcionar

This verb means 'to work' or 'to function' when talking about objects.

No funciona la televisión	The television doesn't work
¿Funciona el ascensor?	Does the lift work?

Note that you cannot use the verb **trabajar** with objects. However, when you are talking about the car, the verb **andar** (literally 'to walk') is usually used. The same verb is used when talking about watches and clocks.

El coche no anda	The car is not working
Este reloj anda muy bien	This watch goes very well

Mucho/s, mucha/s

We saw in the previous section that you use **mucho** for describing a verb.

Estudia mucho   S/he studies a lot

In addition you can use **mucho/a/os/as** with nouns. When this happens it takes the gender and the number of the noun.

Tiene *mucha* **luz**	It is *very* light
Tiene *muchas* **hermanas**	S/he has *a lot* of sisters
Tengo *muchos* **libros de Lorca**	I have *a lot* of books by Lorca
¿Tienes *mucho* **dinero?**	Do you have *a lot* of money?
Este hotel tiene *muchas* **habitaciones**	This hotel has *lots* of rooms

In English you ask for a light when you want to light a cigarette, but in Spanish we use the noun **fuego** (fire).

¿Tienes fuego?	Do you have a light?
¿Tiene fuego?	Do you (formal) have a light?

More adverbs of quantity: *bastante, poco, demasiado* and *nada*

Me gusta *bastante*	I like it *quite a lot*
Me gusta muy *poco*	I like it very *little*
Me gusta *demasiado*	I like it *too much*
No me gusta *nada* **ese piso**	I do not like that flat *at all*

Note that in Spanish two negatives are used together: **no** and **nada**:

No me gusta nada ese vestido	I don't like that dress at all
A mí tampoco	Me neither
No me gusta nada esa falda	I don't like that skirt at all
A mí tampoco	Me neither
Me gusta mucho ese vestido	I like that dress very much
A mí también	Me too
No me gusta mucho esa falda	I don't like that skirt very much
Pues a mí sí	Well, I do
Me gusta mucho Lope de Vega	I like Lope de Vega very much
A mí no me gusta nada	I don't like him at all
Me gustan los cuadros de Dalí	I like Dalí's paintings
A mí, no	I don't

También and **tampoco** are used to register agreement with the statement made by the other speaker. **También** is used when responding to affirmative sentences, and **tampoco** when responding to negative sentences. Notice that because the subject of sentences with the verb **gustar** is the object that is liked, you cannot say in Spanish, 'I like it/them', as in English. You only need to say **me gusta**; you cannot say **me lo gusta**.

¿Te gusta el pescado?	Do you like fish?
Sí, me gusta mucho	Yes, I like it a lot

Nadie/alguien

¿Hay *alguien* en tu casa?	Is there *someone* in your house?
No hay *nadie*	There is *no one*
No hay *nadie* en la fiesta	There is *no one* at the party
¿Vas con *alguien* al teatro?	Are you going with *someone* to the theatre?
No voy con nadie. Voy sola	I am not going with *anybody*. I am going on my own

Remember that in Spanish we often use two negatives together.

The adverb **nunca** also needs the adverb **no** when it goes after the verb.

No voy *nunca* al teatro	I *never* go to the theatre
No como *nunca* antes de la una	I *never* eat before one o'clock

However, when the adverb **nunca** goes before the verb, the adverb **no** is not needed.

Nunca voy al teatro	I *never* go to the theatre
Nunca como antes de la una	I *never* eat before one o'clock

Como

You have already seen the use of **cómo** as an interrogative adverb.

¿Cómo estás?	How are you?
¿Cómo te llamas?	What is your name?

There are many other uses of **como**. You have seen one of them in the dialogue. Here it means 'as':

Como ve, el piso es pequeño *As* you see the flat is small

Another use of **como** is for comparisons:

Soy tan alta *como* mi hermana I am as tall *as* my sister
La hace *como* su madre She makes it *like* her mother

Pronunciation ▮▮

The letter **g** followed by the vowels **a**, **o** or **u** is pronounced strongly. Practise:

gato gorra gustar
Al gato le gusta jugar con la gorra

In order to have the same sound before the vowels **e** or **i** the spelling is different:

guerra guía
El guía murió en la guerra

Language in use

Exercise 8

Respond to the following sentences, agreeing or disagreeing, with your own preferences. If you don't know the person or the film, remember you can say **no la/le conozco**.

1 A mí me gusta mucho Picasso
2 A mí me gustan mucho las películas de Almodóvar
3 A mí no me gusta mucho Dalí
4 A mí no me gusta nada Julio Iglesias
5 A mí me gusta mucho Miró
6 A mí no me gustan mucho las novelas de ciencia ficción
7 Me gusta mucho viajar en tren
8 No me gusta viajar en autobús

Exercise 9

Whilst staying at a friend's house something has gone wrong with some of the appliances in the house. Write a note to your friend telling him/her what the problems are.

Exercise 10

Answer the following questions:

1 ¿Tienes muchos libros españoles?
2 ¿Te gusta mucho el español?
3 ¿Estás muy contenta/o hoy?
4 ¿Tienes muchos discos de cantantes españoles?
5 ¿Escribes mucho?
6 ¿Vas muchas veces a la playa?
7 ¿Eres muy alegre?
8 ¿Trabajas muchas horas?

Exercise 11

Fill in the gaps with **muy** or **mucho/a/os/as**:

1 Tengo _____ amigos en España.
2 Estoy _____ triste porque mi amiga no puede venir.
3 Escribo _____ veces a mis amigos pero ellos no me escriben
   nunca.
4 Me gusta _____ leer libros de ciencia ficción.
5 Luis tiene _____ hermanos.
6 Si quieres aprobar tienes que estudiar _____.
7 'El amor en los tiempos de cólera' es _____ bonito.
8 Carmen Linares canta _____ bien.

Vocabulary building

Exercise 12

Here are some illustrations of furniture or objects found in the
home. Classify them according to where they would go. Some of
them could go in various rooms.

la cocina   el comedor   el dormitorio   el salón   el estudio

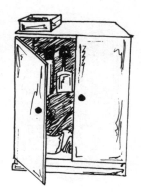

(el) armario

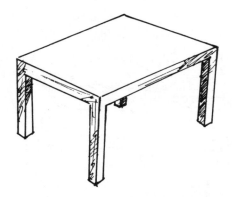

(la) mesa

(la) silla

(la) cocina de gas

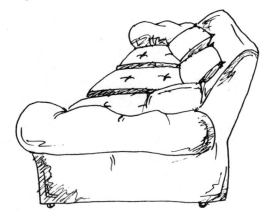

(el) sofá

(la) butaca

(la) mesilla de noche

(la) lámpara

(la) lavadora

(la) librería

(la) cama

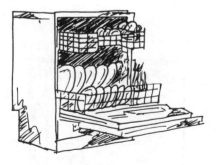

(el) lavavajillas

(el) ordenador

(el) cuadro

(el) espejo

(la) impresora

(la) cómoda

(la) nevera

(el) horno

Exercise 13

Words are sometimes formed by joining a verb with a noun. Take the imperative form of the verb (**tú** form), and simply add the noun.

   e.g.   **abrir** + **latas**   =   **abrelatas**

Form nouns with the following pairs of words:

limpiar	botas
tocar	discos
parar	aguas
parar	brisas
sacar	corchos

Reading

A description of a house

Lesley is living in a friend's house in Mallorca. She describes it to a Spanish person she has met

MARISOL: ¿Vives en un piso o en una casa?
LESLEY: En una casa.
MARISOL: ¿Es grande?
LESLEY: Sí, bastante. Tiene dos plantas. En la primera planta

hay tres dormitorios bastante grandes y un estudio. En la planta baja hay una cocina grande, un comedor y un salón muy grande.

MARISOL: ¿Está cerca de la playa?

LESLEY: Sí, a unos cien metros, pero hay también piscina.

MARISOL: ¡Qué suerte!

LESLEY: Sí, pero no es mía, es de unos amigos que están ahora en Londres.

MARISOL: ¿Hasta cuándo vas a estar?

LESLEY: Hasta julio.

Answer the following questions:

1 Is the house within walking distance of the beach?
2 Which rooms are on the ground floor?
3 Who owns the house?

9 Al teléfono

On the phone

In this lesson we will look at:

- thanking people for things
- making phone calls
- some uses of the preposition **para**
- uses of **ya**
- the verb **dar**
- the present continuous tense

Dialogue 🔲

Phoning a friend

Paul is watching a TV programme that he knows a Spanish friend would enjoy, so he phones her. Her mother answers the phone

MADRE: ¿Diga?
PAUL: Hola, buenas tardes, ¿está Irene?
MADRE: Sí, un momento. Voy a ver lo que está haciendo.
MADRE: Irene, al teléfono.
IRENE: ¿Sí?
PAUL: Hola Irene, soy Paul. Mira, te llamo porque están dando un programa sobre el asesinato de Kennedy.
IRENE: Sí, ya lo sé, lo estoy viendo.
PAUL: Entonces no te molesto. Te llamo después para hablar del programa. ¿Vale?
IRENE: De acuerdo, hasta luego.

Language points

The present continous

This tense needs the verb **estar** plus the gerund (i.e. '-ing' forms like 'eating', 'speaking', 'working', etc.) form of the verb. In order to make the gerund, take the infinitive form of the verb, drop the ending **-ar** and add **-ando**, or for the endings **-er** and **-ir**, add **-iendo**.

Estoy habl*ando* con Juana	I *am* speak*ing* with Juana
¿Estás trabaj*ando*?	*Are* you work*ing*?
Pedro está com*iendo*	Pedro *is* eat*ing*
Estamos cocin*ando*	We *are* cook*ing*
¿Estáis v*iendo* la tele?	*Are* you watch*ing* TV?
Están hac*iendo* los deberes	They *are* do*ing* their homework

In Spanish, this tense is only used when the action is actually happening, in contrast with English when it can sometimes refer to future time (e.g. I'm meeting John this evening). In Spanish, you would use the present tense:

***Voy* al cine esta noche**	*I am going* to the cinema tonight
Mañana *cenamos* en tu casa	Tomorrow *we are eating* at your house
El jueves *me voy* de vacaciones	*I am going* on holiday on Thursday

When a reflexive verb is used, the reflexive pronoun can go before **estar** or joined onto the end of the gerund form:

Me estoy duchando	I am having a shower
Estoy duchándome	I am having a shower

Ya

There are quite a few uses of the adverb **ya** so we will look at some of the most useful ones. **Ya** usually means 'already'.

***Ya* lo sé**	I *already* know that
Lo tiene *ya*	S/he *already* has it

Ya is also used to express an action that is expected:

Ya viene el autobús	The bus is coming
Ya es hora de irnos	It is time for us to leave

It is used very often when someone offers to do something.

Voy a comprar el libro	I am going to buy the book
Ya voy yo	I'll go

Voy a escribir a Sonia	I am going to write to Sonia
Ya lo hago yo si quieres	I'll do it if you want

Ya is also used to express the idea that one has heard or understood:

– **¿Entiendes?**	Do you understand?
– **Ya**	Yes

Used in combination with **que** it can carry the meaning 'since' or 'as':

No va ya que le duele la cabeza	S/he is not going as s/he has a headache
Ya que estás aquí, haz ésto	As you are here, do this

Para

The preposition **para** has many uses, so it will not be possible to look at all of them. In addition, there are difficulties when translating from English to Spanish, as Spanish has two prepositions that could be translated by one in English: **por** and **para**. The best thing to do is to learn the different uses as they appear.

To start, the main use of **para** is when there is a sense of 'final purpose', and 'destination'.

Te llamo para hablar del programa	I am calling to talk about the programme
Este regalo es para Gloria	This present is for Gloria
Está ahorrando para el coche	S/he is saving up for the car

When it is used with a person's name or a personal pronoun, then it takes the meaning of 'in my opinion':

Para mí que Marisol está enferma	In my opinion Marisol is ill

> Spanish culture
>
> You can make national and international phone calls from most telephone boxes (**cabinas telefónicas**). You will find them almost everywhere. You can make a phone call from a **locutorio** or telephone booth even if you do not have Spanish coins. These are places where you can pay for your phone call afterwards. You go into a telephone booth, dial the required number, and when you finish the call the person working there will tell you how much the call is. To make an international call dial 07, wait for the international tone, then continue with the country code and the number minus its initial 0. You have to place the required euro coins (1 euro coin) in the groove at the top of the telephone. They will drop in when someone answers. There are *Telefónica* offices in every town.

Language in use

Exercise 1

Match the questions with their answers:

1 ¿Estáis comiendo?

2 ¿Qué estás leyendo?
3 ¿Están trabajando ahora?

4 ¿Qué estás haciendo?

5 ¿Qué estáis cocinando?

6 ¿Está Pedro viendo la tele?

(a) Estoy trabajando en el ordenador

(b) No, están viendo una película
(c) Sí, estamos comiendo en el jardín

(d) Estoy leyendo un libro de poemas

(e) Sí, creo que está viendo las noticias

(f) Estamos cocinando una paella

Exercise 2

You are staying with a family who are quite busy at the moment, so you want to help them as much as you can, and offer to do everything for them.

e.g. – **Voy a cerrar las ventanas**
       – **Ya las cierro yo**

grabar   to tape
fregar   to do the washing up (the **e** becomes **ie** when conjugated)

1 Voy a echar esta carta
2 Tengo que ir al supermercado
3 Voy a poner la lavadora
4 Tengo que terminar de escribir las invitaciones
5 Voy a abrir la puerta
6 Tengo que grabar la película para Susana
7 Tengo que ir a Correos a comprar sellos
8 Voy a fregar

Exercise 3

You have gone shopping for presents as you are going back home. You have bought many presents: **una camiseta** (t-shirt), **un abanico** (fan), **un libro**, **un bolso**, **un juego de café** (a coffee set), **una cazuela de barro** (earthenware casserole), **un jarrón** (vase). Your friend wants to know who they are for. Write the questions and their answers:

e.g. ¿Para quién es el cinturón?
      El cinturón es para mi hermano

Exercise 4

You are having problems with some things in your apartment. A friend who knows about electrical gadgets has just arrived. Ask him/her to look at the washing machine (**la lavadora**), the television, the iron (**la plancha**), and a lamp (**la lámpara**).

e.g. ¿Ya que estás aquí te importa arreglar el tostador?

Exercise 5 ▣▣

If you have the cassettes, answer the following questions after listening to them.

1 Why does Natalie phone Mario?
2 At what time are they meeting?

Dialogue 🔘

A business phone call

Mr Oliver is in Spain on business. He is phoning Mr López to arrange a meeting

SECRETARIA: *Constructora Mesal*, ¿dígame?
MR OLIVER: ¿Podría hablar con el señor López, por favor?
SECRETARIA: Un momento, por favor ¿de parte de quién?
MR OLIVER: Del señor Oliver, de la compañía *Olympia*.
SECRETARIA: Ahora le pongo.
SECRETARIA: Perdone, señor Oliver, pero el señor López está en una reunión. Si me da su número de teléfono, le llamará después del almuerzo.
MR OLIVER: Estoy en el hotel *María Cristina*. El número es 478 15 73, habitación número 24.
SECRETARIA: Muy bien, ¿hacia las 4 le viene bien?
MR OLIVER: Sí.
SECRETARIA: Muchas gracias por llamar. Adiós.
MR OLIVER: Adiós.

Language points

Del señor López

When you use the term **señor** with the surname, then you need to use the article **el**, and **la** when you are using the term **señora**:

El señor Carrillo está aquí   Mr Carrillo is here
La señora Otaola no está hoy Mrs Otaola is not here today

Remember that the preposition **de** plus the article **el** becomes **del**:

De parte del señor López   From Mr López
De parte de la señora Otaola From Mrs Otaola

However, you do not use the article when you are in conversation.

Perdone, señor Oliver   Excuse me, Mr Oliver

Dar

This verb is only irregular in the first person.

Doy clases en la Universidad	I have classes at the university
¿Dónde das clases?	Where do you have classes?
Manuel siempre da todo	Manuel always gives everything
El chocolate da fuerzas	Chocolate gives you strength
¿Me das tu número de teléfono?	Will you give me your phone number?
¿Por qué no le damos una copa?	Why don't we give him/her a drink?
¿Le dais de comer todos los días?	Do you feed it every day?
Le dan de comer una vez al día	They feed it once a day

Gracias por

When you want to thank someone for doing something then you should use the preposition **por** plus an infinitive:

Gracias por venir	Thanks for coming
Gracias por invitarme	Thanks for inviting me
Gracias por traerlo	Thanks for bringing it

It can also go with a noun.

Gracias por el libro	Thanks for the book
Gracias por la camisa	Thanks for the shirt

Dentro

Dentro on its own is an adverb that means 'inside a place'.

Laura está dentro	Laura is inside (the house)

It is used more often with the preposition **de**, meaning 'inside something'.

Está dentro del armario	It is inside the cupboard
Está dentro de la caja	It is inside the box

Dentro de can be followed by an expression of time, as you have seen in the dialogue.

Le llama dentro de unos minutos	He will call you in a few minutes
Viene dentro de una semana	S/he comes in a week's time

Making a phone call

You will probably have noticed that when Paul introduces himself, he says 'I am . . .'.

Soy Paul	I am Paul
Hola, soy Marta	Hi, it's Marta

Generally, there are two words used when answering the phone:

¿Sí?
¿Dígame?

When you want to know who is calling, you say:

¿De parte de quién?

We use the verb **ponerse** to express 'to come to the phone':

Ahora se pone	S/he is coming now
No puede ponerse	S/he cannot come to the phone

The verb **comunicar** is used to express 'to be engaged'

Está comunicando	It is engaged
Comunica	It is engaged

Pronunciation ▣

We saw in the previous lesson that **gue** and **gui** had a strong sound. The letter **g** followed by the vowels **e** and **i** have a different sound. It sounds like the Spanish **j**. Practise the following:

gente   Gibraltar   gigante   geranio   girasol

Esos girasoles y esos geranios son gigantes
La gente de Gibraltar habla inglés y español

Language in use

Exercise 6

You are having a birthday party, so you have invited some friends to your house. They all bring you presents. When they are leaving thank them for coming and for the gift.

e.g.   Gracias por venir, y gracias también por el libro

Exercise 7

Answer the following questions:

> e.g. ¿A qué hora va a llegar Merche?
> Dentro de una hora más o menos

1 ¿Cuándo vas de vacaciones?
2 ¿Vas a salir enseguida?
3 ¿Cuándo vas a empezar a trabajar?
4 ¿Cuándo vas a empezar a preparar la comida?
5 ¿A qué hora vas a llegar?
6 ¿Cuándo te mudas de casa?

Exercise 8

A Canadian friend of yours does not know how to make a telephone call in Spanish. She heard the following but could not understand the rest. Fill in the gaps for her.
– ¿Dí_____ ?
– Quisiera hablar con la señora Martinez
– Un momento. ¿De_____ de_____?
– De la señora Peer
– Ahora le_____

Exercise 9

Write two telephone dialogues. In the first one you want to speak to Sr. López, and in the second one you want to speak to Sra. Muro.

Vocabulary building

Exercise 10

Here are some uses of the verb **dar**. Try to match them with their synonyms.

1 Dar la enhorabuena   (a) agradecer
2 Dar un paseo   (b) alimentar
3 Dar un grito   (c) gritar
4 Dar alegría   (d) felicitar
5 Dar rabia   (e) alegrarse

6 Dar de comer   (f) enfadarse/rabiar
7 Dar las gracias   (g) pasear

Exercise 11

Here are some expressions with the verb **dar**. Match them with their English equivalents:

1 **Da recuerdos a tu hermano**   (a) I don't mind (one way or the other)
2 **Dar a luz**   (b) I give you my word
3 **Me da de lado lo que dice**   (c) S/he doesn't do any work
4 **Me da igual**   (d) to give birth
5 **Te doy mi palabra**   (e) Give my love/regards to your brother
6 **No da golpe**   (f) I don't care what s/he says

Reading

Rob has gone to the flat of some friends to ask one of them to take him into the centre of town. He feels embarrassed about asking Rosa because he does not know her very well.

1 Why can't Rob go to the centre?
2 Why doesn't Rob want to disturb Luis?
3 What do you think Rosa's profession is?

ROB: ¿Qué está haciendo Lola?
ROSA: Está escribiendo algo en el ordenador ¿pues?
ROB: No, es que necesito ir al centro y tengo el coche averiado. Y Luis ¿está en casa?
ROSA: Sí, pero creo que está estudiando, tiene los exámenes mañana.
ROB: ¡Ah! entonces no le molesto. Y Juanjo ¿no está por aquí?
ROSA: No, lo siento, está trabajando.
ROB: Bueno, pues . . . ah, bueno pues me voy . . .
ROSA: ¿A qué hora tienes que estar allí?
ROB: Antes de las doce.
ROSA: Ya te llevo yo. Pero tienes que esperar un poco, estoy terminando de preparar una lección para esta tarde.
ROB: Muchísimas gracias, no sabes lo que te lo agradezco. Ya sé

que estás muy ocupada. Pero ¿estás segura? No quiero molestarte.

ROSA: Sí, hombre. Si no, no me ofrecería a llevarte.

10 En la oficina

At the office

In this lesson we will look at:

- talking about things you have done
- making excuses
- more imperatives
- the verbs **hay que**, **parece que** and **tocar**
- some more uses of the verb **tener**
- the present perfect tense

Dialogue

At work

Chris started a new office job a few weeks ago. His boss is not too happy about having a man as a secretary, so asks him what he has done that morning in order to find him at fault

JEFE: A ver, dígame lo que ha hecho esta mañana.

CHRIS: Pues he escrito tres cartas, he llamado por teléfono a varios clientes y he hablado con la señora Sánchez sobre las citas de mañana.

JEFE: ¿Eso es todo lo que ha hecho en cuatro horas?

CHRIS: Bueno, también he tenido que ir a la librería a comprar un libro para su esposa.

JEFE: ¡Ah bueno! ¿Y qué libro le ha comprado?

CHRIS: El que me dijo usted, *La Comida Mexicana*.

JEFE: Bueno, eso es todo de momento. Ya sabe que aquí hay que trabajar duro.

CHRIS: Sí señor.

Language points

The present perfect

To form this tense you need to know how the verb **haber** is conjugated. **Haber** is the auxiliary (help verb) used to form this tense. In addition, you drop the infinitive ending **-ar** and add **-ado**, and the endings **-er** and **-ir** and add **-ido**. The participle ('gone', 'eaten', 'danced') does not change.

Hoy *he estudiado* mucho	*I have studied* a lot today
¿*Has comido* algo esta mañana?	*Have you eaten* anything this morning?
Luis *ha salido* hoy muy pronto	Today *Luis has left* very early
Hemos ido esta semana	*We have been* this week
¿*Habéis ido* este año a España?	*Have you been* to Spain this year?
Mis padres *se han ido*	*My parents have gone*

However, there are some irregularities that you should learn as they are used very often.

¿*Has escrito* a Juan?	*Have you written* to Juan?
No *he visto* a nadie	*I haven't seen* anybody
Pedro *ha vuelto* hoy	Pedro *has come back* today
¿Quién *ha abierto* la ventana?	*Who has opened* the window?
Te *he dicho* que no	*I have told* you no
¿Qué *has hecho* hoy?	What *have you done* today?

This past tense is used when the action is finished but the period of time in which this action took place has not finished, or it is very near to the present. That is why you use this tense with expressions such as: **esta semana, este mes, este año, esta mañana, hoy.** When you talk about the things you have done, for example this year, the year has not ended yet.

Este año no ha estudiado nada	S/he has not studied at all this year

In addition, the present perfect is used to talk about past experiences without specifying the time when they happened.

He estado muchas veces en Madrid	I have been to Madrid many times
¿Has leído *El Quijote*?	Have you read *El Quijote*?

It is also used when the action has a strong influence or repercussions in the present.

Perdona por no venir antes pero es que no he tenido tiempo
Excuse me for not coming before, but I haven't had the time

Lo que/el que/la que

There are many uses of the word **que** and it can mean different things in different sentences. In the previous dialogue, the first use of **lo que** refers to all the things Chris has done.

When we do not want or need to specify what we are referring to, then we use the neutral article **lo** in front of **que**. This could be to refer to many things, both masculine and feminine objects, or to refer to a whole sentence.

Lo que dices es cierto	What you are saying is true
Todo lo que ves es de Pedro	Everything you see is Pedro's

In the first sentence **lo que** refers to what the other person is saying, whilst in the second it refers to everything they can see.

However, later on in the dialogue, Chris says:

El que me dijo usted   The one you told me

They both know **el que** refers to the book, therefore it takes the masculine article. If they had been talking about a magazine, **una revista**, then the feminine article would have been used.

La que me dijo usted   The one you told me

Hay que

When **hay** is followed by **que** plus a verb in the infinitive, it means 'to be necessary, or convenient'.

Hay que trabajar mucho	It is necessary to work hard
Hay que ir en coche	It is necessary to go by car
No hay que ir hoy	It is not necessary to go today

Notice that the negative **no** goes in front of the verb **hay** rather than the infinitive.

No hay que escribir el apellido	It is not necessary to write your surname

---

Spanish culture

Although the number of residents has fallen by around 20% in the last few years, many people have gone to Spain looking for a job. In addition to having a residence permit you must obtain a work permit. You have to go to the **Oficina de Extranjeros**. If you only want to work for less than nine months you will need a copy of your passport, six photographs, a copy of the visa application form, a subscription for Social Security, a criminal record document and a work contract.

Many people go to Spain to teach English in a language school. If you want to teach in a reliable school you should have an English-teaching qualification. If you apply for a job from your own country most Spanish schools will obtain the necessary work permit for you.

Language in use

Exercise 1

Match the following questions with their respective answers:

1 ¿Dónde has estado?

2 ¿Con quién has comido?

3 ¿A quién has visto en la fiesta?

4 ¿Adónde has ido esta mañana?

5 ¿Has visto el programa sobre Galicia?

6 ¿Has leído el periódico?

(a) No, he visto uno sobre Toledo

(b) He ido a la embajada

(c) He comido solo

(d) No, todavía no

(e) No he visto a nadie conocido

(f) He estado todo el día en casa

Exercise 2

Look again at the *Language point* on the present perfect tense, and then write down six things you have done this week.

Exercise 3

Your girlfriend/boyfriend is very jealous. S/he has been phoning you all day and you haven't answered the phone. Your bag was stolen so you had to go to the police station and make a few phone calls, etc. Answer her/his questions.

1 ¿A qué hora has salido de casa?
2 ¿Dónde has estado todo el día?
3 ¿Dónde te lo han robado?
4 ¿Qué te han dicho en el cuartel de policía?
5 ¿Has tenido que rellenar muchos papeles?
6 ¿Has llamado a VISA para cancelar la tarjeta?
7 ¿Has ido al banco para cancelar el talón de cheques?

Exercise 4

Here is a list of the things you need to do if you want to pass an exam. Write them in order of importance, according to your experience.

Hay que concentrarse
Hay que ir a las clases
Hay que estudiar mucho
Hay que coger apuntes buenos
Hay que leer libros de consulta
Hay que hacer otras cosas
Hay que hablar sobre los temas con otros estudiantes

Exercise 5

Match the questions with their respective answers:

1 ¿Qué revista has comprado? (a) El que he encontrado en la cocina

2 ¿Qué películas te gustan más? (b) Lo que he visto con mis propios ojos

3 ¿Qué le has dicho? (c) Las que tienen sentido del humor

4 ¿Qué te gustaría para tu cumpleaños? (d) La que siempre compro

5 ¿Qué libro estás leyendo? (e) Lo que de verdad me gustaría serían unas buenas vacaciones

Exercise 6

The woman you are working for asks you if you have done all the things that need doing for the party she is giving for her son. Answer her questions saying that you have already done them.

    e.g.   ¿Has fregado los platos?
            Sí, ya los he fregado

1 ¿Has hecho la compra?
2 ¿Has preparado la mesa?
3 ¿Has comprado las velas para la tarta?
4 ¿Has planchado la camisa nueva?
5 ¿Has preparado los sándwiches?
6 ¿Has llamado a los amigos de Luisito?

Dialogue

Arriving late

Julia is going to a restaurant with some colleagues from work. She is late because her daughter is not feeling well

JULIA: Hola, perdonad por llegar tarde pero es que mi hija se ha puesto enferma esta tarde.

LORENA: Tranquila, mujer ¿Qué tal se encuentra ahora?

JULIA: Un poco mejor. El médico le ha dado un jarabe para la fiebre y parece que le ha bajado un poco.

LUISA: ¿Quién se ha quedado con ella, tu marido?

JULIA: Sí, no le toca trabajar esta noche.

LUISA: Bueno, pues ahora a comer.

JULIA: Sí, tengo una hambre que no veo, no he comido nada desde la mañana.

Perdona por

When you want to excuse yourself to someone then you use the preposition **por** plus an infinitive, the same as **gracias por**.

Perdona por llegar tarde	Excuse me for being late
Perdona por no escribirte antes	Excuse me for not writing before
Perdone por llegar tarde	Excuse me (formal) for arriving (being) late

You will probably have noticed that Julia says **perdonad** rather than **perdona**. This is because she is talking to more than one person. The imperative ending for more than one person is **-ad** for **-ar** verbs, **-ed** for **-er** verbs, and **-id** for **-ir** verbs.

Tomad la leche	Have (drink) the milk
Perdonad por llegar tarde	Excuse me for being late
Comed todo	Eat everything
Id al cine	Go to the cinema
Venid mañana	Come tomorrow

However, in colloquial language, you will hear people using the infinitive instead of the second person plural form of the imperative.

Perdonar por llegar tarde	Excuse me for being late
Sentaros	Sit down

Instead of

Sentaos	Sit down

Notice that the second person plural form **lavad** loses the **d** when the verb is a reflexive one.

Lavad la ropa	Wash the clothes
Lavaos la cara	Wash your face

Tener *as 'to be'*

In Spanish, we use this verb in many instances when in English the verb 'to be' is used.

Tengo hambre	I am hungry
¿Tienes sed?	Are you thirsty?
¿Tienes frío?	Are you cold?
Tengo mucho calor	I am very hot
Tengo mucha suerte	I am very lucky
Rosario tiene sueño	Rosario is tired
Tienes razón	You are right
¿Tienes prisa?	Are you in a hurry?
¿Tienes miedo?	Are you frightened?

Although the word **hambre** is feminine, the masculine article is used in front of the word because words that start with a strong **a/ha** (i.e. that syllable is pronounced the strongest within the word) take the masculine article regardless of whether they are feminine or masculine.

El agua está fría	*The water* is cold
¿Dónde está *el hacha*?	Where is *the axe*?

Notice that although they take a masculine article the adjectives that describe those objects are feminine.

El agua está *templada*	The water is tepid

There are, however, some exceptions:

La hache está al principio	The 'h' is at the beginning

Parece que

We have seen in previous lessons the use of *parecer* with indirect pronouns.

Me parece bien	I think it is OK/ I agree

You can use the same verb followed by **que**, and without the pronoun, to indicate that 'there are signs of something'.

Parece que le ha bajado la fiebre	It seems like his temperature has come down
Parece que va a llover	It looks like it is going to rain

When the verb goes with the indirect pronoun it means 'to think'.

Me parece que estudia muy poco	I think s/he studies very little
¿Te parece que va a venir?	Do you think s/he is going to come?

¿Quién? *(Who?)*

The interrogative pronouns **quién/quiénes** do not usually cause any problems to the English speaker. However, you must use the plural form when 'who' refers to more than one person:

¿Quién se queda con él?	Who is staying with him?
¿Quiénes van al cine?	Who is going to the cinema?

Tocar

This verb has many uses. When it is conjugated as a normal verb it means 'to play a musical instrument'.

Toco el piano bastante bien	I play the piano quite well
¿Sabes tocar la guitarra?	Can you play the guitar?

It can also mean 'to touch':

¿Por qué te tocas el ojo?	Why are you touching your eye?
No lo toques	Don't touch it

However, when it is conjugated like the verb **gustar**, it means 'to be one's turn to do something'.

Me toca a mí	It's my turn
¿Te toca a ti?	Is it your turn?
No le toca trabajar esta noche	It is not his turn to work tonight
¿A quién le toca fregar hoy?	Whose turn is it to do the washing up today?
Le toca a Juan	It is Juan's turn

Two negatives do not make a positive

Remember that Spanish differs from English in that it uses two negative adverbs together.

No **he comido** *nada* **desde esta mañana**	I have*n't* eaten *anything* since this morning
No **me gusta** *nada*	I do*n't* like it *at all*
¿Hay algo en la nevera?	Is there *anything* in the fridge?
Creo que *no* **hay** *nada*	I do*n't* think there is *anything*

We also saw two negatives used together in Lesson 8.

No **he visto a** *nadie*	I have*n't* seen *anybody*
No **hay** *nadie* **en casa**	There is *nobody* at home

Pronunciation

Although in the previous lesson we saw the sounds of the syllables **ge** and **gi**, there are words that despite having the same sound, are spelled differently; they are spelled with the letter **j** (**jota**). There is no rule so you have to learn the different spellings as you learn the words.

jefe	but	**general**
Jijona	but	**Gijón**

Before the vowels **a**, **o** and **u** the **j** (**jota**) is always used:

José Juan jamón
El jefe de Gijón es general
A José y a Juan les gusta comer jamón

Language in use

Exercise 7

Match the following questions with their respective answers:

1	¿Venimos el lunes?	(a) No, subidla al cuarto piso
2	¿Comemos aquí?	(b) No, ponedlos en la mesa
3	¿Venís con nosotros?	(c) No, traed pasteles
4	¿Abrimos la tienda ahora?	(d) No, comed en el jardín
5	¿Ponemos los libros en la librería?	(e) No, id vosotros solos
6	¿Dejamos la televisión en la mesa?	(f) No, abridla más tarde
7	¿La subimos al tercer piso?	(g) No, dejadla en el suelo
8	¿Traemos vino?	(h) No, venid el martes

Exercise 8

Here are a parent's answers to the complaints made by his/her son. What were the complaints?

1 Pues vete a la cama
2 Pues come un bocadillo
3 Pues ponte un jersey
4 Pues quítate la chaqueta
5 Pues bebe un vaso de agua
6 Pues sal ya

Exercise 9

You have not had a good week, and you have not done the things you ought to have done. Make your excuses, giving a different reason for each one.

1 Perdona por llegar tarde pero es que . . .
2 Perdona por no llamar antes pero . . .

3 Perdona por no escribirte antes . . .
4 Perdona por no ir . . .
5 Perdona por llamar tan tarde . . .
6 Perdona por no cocinar hoy . . .

Exercise 10

You share a flat with a group of friends. In the morning you usually discuss whose turn it is to do things. Write down the questions you would ask in that situation, and their answers.

> e.g   **¿A quién le toca hacer la compra?**
> **Le toca a Pedro**

Exercise 11

A friend of yours whose Spanish is not very good has asked you to translate the card she has just received from a Spanish friend who is coming to stay with her.

Querida Jude:

Muchas gracias por la invitación, pero no voy a poder ir porque mi madre se ha puesto enferma y va a tener que quedarse en el hospital unas semanas. Yo, como siempre, tengo que cuidar a mis hermanos. Perdona por todo. Si no te importa podría ir en Semana Santa, ¿qué te parece? Escríbeme pronto.

Un abrazo

Vocabulary building

Exercise 12

Here are some expressions with the verb **tener**. Can you match them with their English equivalents?

1	**Tengo una hambre que no veo**	(a)	S/he always agrees with me
2	**Manolo se cae de sueño**	(b)	I am going to try my luck
3	**Siempre me da la razón**	(c)	I'm starving
4	**Me ahogo/muero de calor**	(d)	S/he is always hurrying me up
5	**Voy a probar la suerte**	(e)	I am boiling hot
6	**Siempre me mete prisa**	(f)	Manolo is falling asleep on his feet

Exercise 13

Many words in Spanish have an **e** before the combination of **s** and another consonant. Many of them are very similar to their English equivalents. Can you match them?

1	**especialista**	(a)	strict
2	**estómago**	(b)	spy
3	**escapar**	(c)	specialist
4	**estéril**	(d)	scene/stage
5	**estricto**	(e)	scandal
6	**espontáneo**	(f)	stable
7	**escenario**	(g)	stomach
8	**espiar**	(h)	escape
9	**estable**	(i)	spontaneous
10	**escándalo**	(j)	sterile

Reading

Natalia arrives home late one evening. Daniel, her husband, is upset because he wanted to go out for a drink with her
Read the dialogue and answer the following questions:

1 Why didn't Natalia phone him?
2 Why is Pepa upset?
3 Where is Pepa's boyfriend?

NATALIA: Perdona por llegar tarde
DANIEL: ¿Dónde has estado?
NATALIA: Cuando he salido del trabajo he ido a ver la película de Saura
DANIEL: ¿Por qué no me has llamado cuando has salido? Podíamos haber ido a tomar una copa juntos. Hace

tiempo que no hemos salido.

NATALIA: Es que cuando ha terminado la película me he encontrado con Pepa.

DANIEL: ¡Ah! Así que ella es más importante que yo ¿no?

NATALIA: No hombre, pero es que ha roto con su novio y está bastante mal.

DANIEL: Ah lo siento, no lo sabía. ¿Cuándo han roto?

NATALIA: Esta semana. Creo que él se ha ido a vivir con su hermana en Sevilla. Se ha llevado todo, hasta el coche.

DANIEL: ¡Pobre Pepa!

Exercise 14

Here is a list of six things to help stop cars polluting the environment. Place them in order of importance.

1 Se puede ir en tren, autobús, o bicicleta
2 Mantenga el coche a punto
3 Cambie los filtros y el aceite periódicamente
4 Mantenga una velocidad de crucero prudente
5 No lave el coche más que lo imprescindible
6 Si tiene que utilizar el coche, compártalo con otras personas

11 Problemas familiares

Family problems

In this lesson we will look at:

- the preterite tense
- how to express concern
- how to agree to something
- the verbs **volver a** and **costar**

Dialogue 🔲

Asking for news

Peter and his brother went to Spain to work as English teachers. Peter's brother, Simon, had a terrible row with his brother and family and has not been in contact with them since. Peter meets a Spanish friend of Simon's at a party

PETER: ¡Hola Merche! ¡Qué sorpresa verte por aquí! ¿Cómo te va todo?

MERCHE: Hola Peter, muy bien y ¿a ti?

PETER: Pues regular. Estoy muy preocupado por mi hermano. Por cierto, no le habrás visto últimamente, ¿no?

MERCHE: Pues no, la última vez creo que fue en la fiesta de cumpleaños de Roberto. Vino con Manola. Mira está ahí ¿por qué no le preguntas a ella? Igual sabe algo.

PETER: Sí, voy ahora mismo. Hasta luego.

PETER: Perdona Manola, ¿Has visto a Simon últimamente?

MANOLA: Hablé con él ayer, ¿pues?

PETER: Es que no sé nada de él desde hace mucho tiempo.

Discutimos un día y desde entonces no le he vuelto a ver.
¿Qué tal está?

MANOLA: Bien, creo, no me dijo nada especial.

PETER: Si te llama otra vez por favor dile que mis padres y yo
estamos muy preocupados.

MANOLA: Vale, ya se lo digo, pero tranquilo, hombre, no te preocupes.

Language in use

The preterite tense

This tense is used to express an action completed at a definite time
in the past. For this reason this tense is used with expressions of
time such as **ayer**, **anoche** (last night), **la semana pasada**, **el mes
pasado**, **el año pasado**, **hace dos días**, etc.

When Merche talks about the last time she saw Simon, she uses
the preterite tense because the action happened at a specific time in
the past.

The preterite for **-ar** regular verbs is formed by dropping the
infinitive ending **-ar** and adding the following endings:

Hablé con él ayer	*I spoke* with him yesterday
¿Hablaste con ella?	*Did you speak* with her?
Habló con la madre	*S/he spoke* with the mother
Hablamos con ellos	*We spoke* with them
¿Hablasteis de ella?	*Did you speak* about her?
Hablaron de la película	*They spoke* about the film

In the previous dialogue, however, there are quite few irregular
verbs which are used often.

Ser/Ir

These two verbs have the same form in the preterite tense. The
meaning of the verb can be understood from the context. You will
probably use it most frequently as 'to go', as the verb **ser** is used less
often in the preterite.

Ayer *fui* al cine	*I went* to the cinema yesterday
¿Adónde *fuiste* el año pasado?	Where *did you go* last year?

Ayer Pedro *fue* **muy malo**	Pedro *was* very naughty yesterday
El mes pasado *fuimos* **a París**	Last month *we went* to Paris
¿Adónde *fuisteis* **anoche?**	Where *did you go* last night?
Se fueron **de vacaciones**	*They went* on holiday

Tener

El mes pasado *tuve* **mucho trabajo**	Last month *I had* lots of work
¿*Tuviste* **frío anoche?**	*Were you* cold last night?
El año pasado *tuvo* **mucha suerte**	Last year *s/he was* very lucky
Anoche *tuvimos* **que coger un taxi**	Last night *we had* to take a taxi
¿*Tuvisteis* **que hablar con él?**	*Did you have* to talk to him?
Tuvieron **que irse antes**	*They had* to leave earlier

Volver a

When this verb is used with the preposition **a** and an infinitive it means 'to do again' or 'to repeat' whatever is expressed by the verb in the infinitive.

Ha vuelto a suspender	S/he has failed again
¿Has vuelto a ir?	Have you been again?
¿Has vuelto a verle?	Have you seen him again?

Igual

The word **igual** normally means 'the same':

Loren es igual que su padre	Loren is the same as his father

Used as in the dialogue, however, it means 'perhaps':

Igual sabe algo	Perhaps she knows something
Igual viene más tarde	Perhaps s/he will come later
Igual me voy a Vitoria	Perhaps I will go to Vitoria

This is very useful as the word **quizás** (perhaps) takes the subjunctive mood in Spanish, which will be discussed later.

Se lo

We have seen the use of direct and indirect object pronouns. Remember that direct and indirect object pronouns only differ in the third person: **lo/los/le**, **la/las** for direct objects, and **le/les** for indirect objects.

La **veo todos los días**	I see *her* everyday
Siempre compra las camisas allí	S/he always buys *shirts* there
Siempre *las* **compra allí**	S/he always buys *them* there
¿Has comprado ya el libro?	Have you already bought *the book*?
¿*Lo* **has comprado ya?**	Have you already bought *it*?
Le **di un libro**	I gave *him/her* a book

When there are two objects, a direct and an indirect one, the indirect object pronoun always precedes the direct object pronoun.

Spanish culture

The areas that attract the most tourists are the Balearic Islands, the Canaries, and the coastal areas of Alicante and Málaga. The coast of Galicia in the north-west and Asturias are still relatively unspoilt. However, the **rías bajas** and **rías altas**, together with the fabulous seafood, make Galicia an area worth discovering. San Sebastián in the Basque Country and Santander have for a long time been traditional holiday places for Spanish people.

The **Costa Brava** in Cataluña covers the area from Blanes to Port-Bou. Some of its most famous places are Lloret de Mar, San Feliú de Guixols, Palamós, and Gerona. Barcelona, the capital of Cataluña, is a city full of culture and history. The **Costa del Azahar** on the east coast takes its name from the beautiful white blossom of the orange trees. It has many historical towns such as Castellón, Sagunto, and Valencia.

The area of Alicante and Murcia is called the **Costa Blanca**. Málaga is the capital of the **Costa del Sol**. Some of the most popular places on the **Costa del Sol** are Marbella, Nerja, and Torremolinos. Cádiz and Huelva form what is called the **Costa de la Luz**. In this area you can visit El Coto de Doñana, a nature reserve where you can see mongooses and a wide variety of birds, including flamingoes. The **Islas Baleares** and the **Islas Canarias** attract millions of tourists. There are, in addition, hundreds of places to visit in the interior: Estella, Santo Domingo de la Calzada, Burgos, Salamanca, Segovia, Ávila, Toledo, Granada, Sevilla, Córdoba. Cáceres, and Badajoz are some of the most magnificent historical towns.

Te di el libro ayer	I gave you the book yesterday
Te lo di ayer	I gave it to you yesterday
¿Cuándo me lo diste?	When did you give it to me?
Te lo di el lunes	I gave it to you on Monday
Nos lo dio el martes	He gave it to us on Tuesday

Note that when an indirect object is used with a direct object, the indirect objects **le** and **les** both change to **se**:

¿Cuándo le diste el libro?	When did you give him/her the book?
Se lo di el miércoles	I gave it to him/her on Wednesday

> **¿Cuándo le diste la revista?**   When did you give him/her the
>   magazine?
> **Se la di el jueves**   I gave it to him/her on Thursday

Note that **le lo** and **le la** can never go together.

Language in use

Exercise 1

Match the questions with their respective answers:

1	¿Cuándo le diste los deberes?	(a)	Me la dieron ayer
2	¿Cuándo se lo compraste?	(b)	Se lo dije ayer
3	¿Cuándo le diste la carta?	(c)	Se los di el viernes
4	¿Cuándo le diste el paquete?	(d)	Se la di el jueves
5	¿Cuándo le dijiste eso?	(e)	Se lo compré ayer
6	¿Cuándo te dieron la noticia?	(f)	Se lo di la semana pasada

Exercise 2

Answer the following questions using the appropriate direct and indirect object pronouns:

1 ¿Cuándo compraste los billetes?
2 ¿Cuándo viste a Mario?
3 ¿Cuándo le diste el libro?
4 ¿Cuándo le mandaste el regalo?
5 ¿Quién te compró esa pulsera?
6 ¿Cuándo construyeron la casa?

Exercise 3

Answer the following questions:

¿Adónde fuiste ayer?
¿Fuiste ayer a clase de español?
¿Bebiste algo diferente ayer?
¿Comiste solo/a ayer?
¿Fuiste al cine la semana pasada?
¿Adónde fuiste de vacaciones el año pasado?

Exercise 4

It is the New Year and as usual you think of things you would like to do in the following months. List six things you may do.

> e.g. **Este año igual aprendo a conducir**   This year I may learn how to drive

Exercise 5

Sara wanted to go to a conference that a leading professor was giving in Barcelona. However, it was not to be. She has written a few sentences about her disastrous journey, but they have all become muddled. Can you put them in the correct order?

No puedes imaginarte qué desastre de viaje. Tardó en arreglarlo más de dos horas. Una mujer muy simpática paró pero en medio del camino el coche se averió. Perfecto: la conferencia empezaba a las diez, pero no. ¡Después de todo, la conferencia se había cancelado porque el conferenciante estaba enfermo! Conseguimos un mecánico aunque eran las doce de la noche. Por fin volvimos a la carretera. Perdí el último tren así que tuve que ir a dedo. Llegamos a Barcelona a las nueve y media.

Exercise 6

Write a short dialogue between two friends. One of them wants to know if the other has seen again the two people they met a few weeks ago. She saw them last week, and they went for a drink together.

Exercise 7

An American friend of yours wants to write a card in Spanish. She does not know how to use the past tense so you have offered to help her. Correct the tenses as necessary.

Hola Sonia:

¿Cómo te va todo? Estoy ahora en un pueblo cerca de Bilbao. La semana pasada estoy con los amigos de Luisa. Voy con ellos a Lequeitio, ¿lo conoces? Es un pueblo pesquero muy bonito. Comemos muchísimas gambas. Ya sabes cuánto me gustan. Después me llevan a las fiestas de Bermeo ¡Qué fiestas! Estamos allí hasta las seis de la mañana.

Hasta pronto,

un abrazo

Dialogue

Passing on a message

Simon phones Manola. She tells him what his brother has said to her. She asks him to phone his brother

MANOLA: ¿Sí?

SIMON: Hola Manola, soy Simon.

MANOLA: ¡Simon, por fin! ¿Cómo estás?

SIMON: Bien, ¿pero por qué dices 'por fin'? Quedamos en que te llamaría hoy ¿no?

MANOLA: Sí, ya sé, pero es que el otro día vi a tu hermano y me dijo que estaba muy preocupado por ti.

SIMON: ¡Ah ya! ¿Te dijo por qué?

MANOLA: Sí, me dijo que discutisteis hace tiempo.

SIMON: Bueno, fue más que una discusión, pero en fin, es problema nuestro.

MANOLA: ¿Vas a llamarle?

SIMON: No sé.

MANOLA: Pero hombre, es tu hermano. No te cuesta nada llamarle.

SIMON: Bueno, bueno, igual le llamo luego.

Language in use

Quedar en

We saw in Lesson 6 that the verb **quedar** had the meaning of 'arranging to meet':

> **Quedé con él en el bar**   I arranged to meet him in the bar

When **quedar** is followed by the preposition **en** plus an infinitive, it means 'to agree on something':

> **Quedamos en vernos hoy**   We agreed to see each other today
> **¿Quedaste en ir?**   Did you agree to go?
> **Pepe quedó en preparar todo**   Pepe agreed to prepare everything

When **quedar en** is followed by **que**, then instead of the infinitive, the conditional is used:

> **Quedamos en que te llamaría hoy**   We agreed that I would phone you today
> **Quedamos en que yo lo haría**   We agreed that I would do it
> **Quedaron en que ellos lo harían**   They agreed that they would do it

Ver

Regular **-er** and **-ir** verbs have the same endings in the preterite form. To form the preterite of these verbs take the **-er** or **-ir** off the infinitive and add the following endings:

> **V*i* una película muy buena ayer**   *I saw* a very good film yesterday
> **¿*Viste* ayer a Juan?**   *Did you see* Juan yesterday?
> **V*io* a Pedro en la piscina**   *S/he saw* Pedro in the swimming pool
> **Le *vimos* ayer**   *We saw* him yesterday
> **¿Les *visteis* el sábado?**   *Did you see* them on Saturday?
> **Les *vieron* el jueves**   *They saw* them on Friday

Costar

This verb normally means 'to cost'. However, when it is used with an indirect object, it means 'to have difficulty in doing something'.

Le cuesta aprender los verbos	S/he finds it hard to learn the verbs
No te cuesta nada llamarle	You can easily phone him now
No me cuesta nada hacerlo	I can do it without any problem
¿Te va a costar hacerlo?	Is it going to be hard for you to do it?
No me cuesta nada ir ahora	I can easily go now

Estar preocupado por

Normally the verb **preocuparse** (to worry) and **estar preocupado** are followed by the preposition **por**:

Estoy preocupado por él	I am worried about him
No te preocupes por ella	Don't worry about her
Se preocupa por todo	S/he worries about everything

However, it is very often followed by the preposition **de**.

Preocúpate de tus asuntos	Mind your own business

Pronunciation 〔○○〕

All Spanish words of more than one syllable have one syllable that is stronger than the others. Some of them have accents according to spelling rules. There are many instances in which this accent helps to show the meaning of the word.

fábrica	fabrica	fabri**có**
célebre	celebre	cele**bré**

You should always pronounce the accented syllable more strongly.

Práctico   **úl**timo   **pró**ximo

En esa fábrica se fabrican piezas
El célebre actor celebró su cumpleaños ayer
El próximo y el último pueden irse

Language in use

Exercise 8

You seem to have misunderstood some arrangements this week. Some of your friends phone you. Tell them what you thought the arrangement was. Remember that the first person of the conditional tense of **decir** is **diría** and of **hacer** is **haría**.

e.g. AMIGA: ¿Por qué no fuiste ayer?
TÚ: Quedamos en que iría hoy ¿no?

Do the same with the rest of the questions:

1 ¿Por qué no me llamaste ayer?
2 ¿Por qué no le has escrito todavía ?
3 ¿Por qué no se lo has dicho todavía?
4 ¿Por qué no hablaste con él ayer?
5 ¿Por qué no has ido esta mañana?
6 ¿Por qué no lo has hecho?

Exercise 9

Answer the following questions:

1 ¿Viste a tus padres ayer?
2 ¿Viste la semana pasada alguna película?
3 ¿Viste a algún amigo ayer?
4 ¿Viste a alguna persona famosa el año pasado?
5 ¿Viste las noticias ayer en la tele?

Exercise 10

Match the following sentences:

1 No me apetece hacerlo   (a) No te cuesta nada ir a verle
2 No me apetece hablar con (b) No te cuesta nada escribir una
   nadie   postal
3 No me apetece salir   (c) No te cuesta nada llamarle hoy
4 No me apetece escribir   (d) No te cuesta nada salir un rato
5 No me apetece ver a nadie (e) Venga hombre, no te cuesta
                                 nada hacerlo hoy

Exercise 11

Answer the following questions:

1 ¿Qué te cuesta más: hablar o escribir español?
2 ¿Qué te cuesta más: aprender los verbos o las preposiciones?
3 ¿Qué te cuesta más: escribir a máquina o escribir a mano?
4 ¿Qué te cuesta más: entender o hablar español?

Vocabulary building

Exercise 12

You saw in the first dialogue that Peter uses the expression **por cierto** (by the way) to change the subject, because he wants to ask about his brother. Here are other expressions that take the preposition **por**. Match them with their English equivalents:

1	Por casualidad	(a)	At last
2	Por si (acaso)	(b)	Therefore
3	Por suerte	(c)	Because of that
4	Por lo demás	(d)	Nearly
5	Por eso	(e)	By chance
6	Por lo tanto/por consiguiente	(f)	Just in case
7	Por fin	(g)	Besides that
8	Por poco	(h)	Luckily

Fill in the gaps with one of the expressions from above:

1 La semana ya se ha pasado, _____ debes volver al médico.
2 Voy a llamarle de nuevo, _____ está enfermo.
3 La vi el otro día _____.
4 Pepe está cansado pero _____ se encuentra bien.
5 He perdido el tren, _____ llego tarde.
6 _____ están bien todos, gracias.
7 ¡_____ llegas!
8 _____ pierdo el autobús.

Reading

Here is a short passage about the life of Miguel de Cervantes, author of Don Quijote de la Mancha

Miguel de Cervantes nació en Alcalá de Henares, en 1547. Vivió con su familia en Valladolid, Madrid y varias ciudades andaluzas. A los veintidós años se fue a Italia como camarero del cardenal Acquaviva. Fue después soldado, y luchó en Lepanto (1571) contra los turcos. Cuatro años más tarde los turcos apresaron su barco. Permaneció cautivo en Argel cinco años (1575–1580). Fue rescatado por los frailes Trinitarios y se instaló en Madrid.

A los treinta y siete años tuvo una hija natural, Isabel, y se casó con Catalina de Salazar; su convivencia fue pronto imposible. En 1605 se instaló en Valladolid y publicó el *Quijote*. Por un asunto oscuro, en el que murió un hombre, fue encarcelado con su hermana y su hija. Los tres fueron absueltos. En 1608 se instalaron en Madrid donde vivieron en la pobreza. Murió el 23 de abril de 1616 (día en que también falleció William Shakespeare).

1 What were some of Cervantes' jobs?
2 Why did he spend some time in Algeria?
3 Was his marriage to Catalina a happy one?

You are writing to a Spanish person for the first time. Tell them something about your life.

12 Escribiendo a casa

Writing home

In this lesson we will look at:
- how to write postcards and formal letters
- talking about the weather
- expressing comparisons
- more on the past
- the verb **tardar**

A postcard 🔲

Peter is spending some time in the north of Spain after having been to see a Spanish friend in Valencia. He sends her a postcard

5 de julio de 1994

Querida Sara:

Como puedes ver por la postal ya estoy en Santander. Llegué hace una semana pero es tan bonito que creo que me voy a quedar hasta finales de mes. Ayer estuve en la playa del Sardinero pero no me bañé porque hacía mucho viento (¡No, no hace frío todos los días!) Anteayer hizo muchísimo calor pero me fui a ver las cuevas de Altamira y me asé de calor. Por cierto, me hablaste tanto de la literatura española que esta mañana me he matriculado en la universidad para hacer un curso de literatura contemporánea. No, si al final seré un experto en España... Bueno ahora me voy a tomar una cerveza ¡Ah! Igual te llamo antes de marcharme. Hasta pronto   Un abrazo

Language points

Estar

Although it is irregular, the preterite tense of **estar** is very similar to the preterite of the verb **tener**. The only thing you must do is to add **es** to the beginning of the verb.

El año pasado *estuve* **en México**	Last year *I was* in Mexico
¿Dónde *estuviste* **ayer?**	Where *were you* yesterday?
Manolo *estuvo* **ayer aquí**	Manolo *was* here yesterday
El sábado *estuvimos* **con Juan**	*We were* with Juan on Saturday
¿Dónde *estuvisteis* **el domingo?**	Where *were you* on Sunday?
Sus padres *estuvieron* **conmigo**	His parents *were* with me

Llegué

Remember that in order to make the **g** sound strong in front of an **e** or **i** it must be followed by **u**.

Llegué ayer	I arrived yesterday
¿Cuándo llegaste?	When did you arrive?

El tiempo *(the weather)*

Spanish uses the verb **hacer** with expressions about the weather.

¿Qué tiempo hace en el centro?	*What is the weather like* in the centre?
En Madrid *hace frío* en invierno	In Madrid *it is cold* in winter
En verano *hace mucho* calor en Sevilla	In summer *it is* very *hot* in Sevilla
¿Hace buen tiempo en tu país?	*Is there good weather* in your country?
Normalmente en Londres hace mal tiempo	*There is* usually *bad weather* in London
En el sur casi todo el año hace sol	*It is sunny* nearly all year in the south
En invierno siempre *nieva* en la sierra	*It* always *snows* in winter in the sierra

En otoño *hace* mucho *viento*	In the autumn *it is* very *windy*
En primavera *llueve* bastante	In spring *it rains* quite a lot

Tan

You have already learned the expressions **tan tarde** and **tan pronto**.

¿Por qué vienes tan tarde?	Why do you come so late?
¿Cómo así vienes tan pronto?	How is it you come so early?

The adverb **tan** can also be used in exclamations:

¡Qué niño tan guapo!	What a pretty child!
Es tan bonito aquí que creo que me voy a quedar	It is so pretty here that I think I will stay
Es tan caro que creo que no puedo comprarlo	It is so expensive that I don't think I can buy it

Tanto/a

This is normally followed by **como** to make comparisons:

No gana tanto como su hermano	S/he doesn't earn as much as her/his brother
No llueve tanto como dicen	It doesn't rain as much as they say
Trabajo tanto como tú	I work as much as you do
Ella tiene tanta paciencia como tú	She has as much patience as you

Note that **tanto** agrees with the noun it modifies. **Tanto** is, however, very often used without **como** to mean 'so much'.

Me hablaste tanto de la literatura española que ...
You talked to me so much about Spanish literature that ...

¡Me acordé tanto de ti!	I thought about you so much!
¡Me divertí tanto!	I enjoyed myself so much!

A finales de

If you don't want to talk about a specific time of the week, month, year, etc., you can use the following expressions:

A finales de año me caso
I am getting married at the end of the year

A mediados de este mes me voy a Lugo
I am going to Lugo around the middle of this month

A principios del mes que viene voy a empezar a estudiar
At the beginning of next month I am going to start studying

Pronunciation/intonation 📼

When you want to make a statement of fact (**Está comiendo** S/he is eating), the information follows this pattern:

TONO ········· NORMAL   ENUNCIATIVA (*declarative*)

If you want to use the same words to ask a question, then the pattern of this information changes as follows:

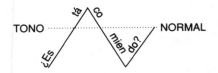

TONO ········· NORMAL   INTERROGATIVA (*interrogative*)

On the other hand, if you want to express surprise, the tone falls at the end of an exclamation:

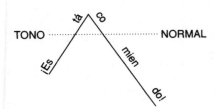

TONO ········· NORMAL   EXCLAMATIVA (*exclamative*)

Spanish culture

The Spanish climate varies enormously from region to region. In the north-west of the peninsula, Galicia, Asturias, and the Basque Country, winters are not very cold and the summers are not too hot. The average temperature in San Sebastián, for example, ranges from 8°C in January to 21°C in August. It rains a lot throughout the year, although rainfall is lower in the summer. The rain in this area is normally quite light but constant. This is known as **llovizna**, **calabobos**, or **sirimiri**. On the Mediterranean coast the temperatures do not vary greatly although they are higher than on the Atlantic coast. They have mild winters. The rain is irregular and infrequent, but stormy, causing floods. The climate in the centre of Spain is characterised by its extreme temperatures; it is very hot in the summer and bitterly cold in winter.

Language in use

Exercise 1

Answer the following questions:

1 ¿Estuviste ayer con tu mejor amigo?
2 ¿Con quién estuviste el domingo?
3 ¿Estuvo tu madre en tu casa la semana pasada?
4 ¿Estuviste muy enfermo/a el año pasado?
5 ¿Quién estuvo en tu casa la semana pasada?

Exercise 2

You are thinking of travelling around Spain in March and April. You are considering going to San Sebastián, Asturias, the centre, and the south. You want to know what kind of weather to expect. Ask a Spanish friend of yours about the climate in these places.

    e.g. ¿Qué tiempo hace normalmente en Salamanca en abril?
         ¿Hace calor en el norte?

Exercise 3

Whilst in Spain you have been asked to describe the weather in your country. Write a few sentences about it.

Exercise 4

Tick any of the following statements which apply to you.

1 Normalmente cobro a principios de mes.
2 Siempre cobro a finales de mes.
3 Normalmente no me queda nada de dinero a finales de mes.
4 A principios de cada mes voy al banco.
5 Normalmente compro la ropa a principios de mes.
6 Siempre como en casa a finales de mes.
7 A principios de año siempre quiero hacer muchas cosas nuevas.
8 Mando las tarjetas de navidad a mediados de diciembre.

Exercise 5

Match the following sentences:

1 He oído hablar tanto de esa película
2 He gastado tanto en las vacaciones
3 He comido tanto
4 He bebido tanto
5 Me has hablado tanto de ese libro
6 He estudiado tanto

(a) que no puedo moverme.
(b) que no puedo ver.
(c) que no me queda ni un duro.
(d) que tengo que aprobar.
(e) que tengo que ir a verla.
(f) que he tenido que comprarlo.

Exercise 6

Write a postcard to a Spanish friend of yours.

A formal letter

Mike Land and his wife bought a rug and some vases in a shop in Spain while they were on holiday. They decided to have them sent to their home. However, they have not yet arrived, so he sends a letter to the shop owner

15 de enero de 1994

Estimado Señor:

Hace algo más de dos meses mi mujer y yo compramos en su tienda una alfombra y unos jarrones que usted prometió mandar la semana siguiente a más tardar. Según dijo usted los artículos tardarían en llegar unas tres semanas. Han pasado ya dos meses y no hemos recibido aún nada. La alfombra es un regalo de boda para mi hija que se va a casar dentro de tres semanas, así que como usted comprenderá estamos muy preocupados por si no llegan a tiempo.

Le agradecería una pronta respuesta.

Le saluda atentamente,

Language points

Aún

With an accent this word is an adverb and it means 'yet' or 'still':

¿Aún no ha llegado Lola?	Hasn't Lola arrived yet?
No ha comido aún	S/he has not eaten yet

This adverb has the same meaning as **todavía**:

¿Todavía no has comido?	Haven't you eaten yet?
¿Ha llegado Manuel?	Has Manuel arrived?
Todavía no/Aún no	Not yet

Without an accent **aun** is a conjunction and it means 'even'.

Aun en invierno lleva sandalias Even in winter she wears sandals

Tardar

This verb means 'to take' when it refers to time.

¿Vas a tardar mucho?	Are you going to take long?
He tardado una hora en escribir la carta	I have taken an hour to write the letter

| ¿Cuánto tiempo se tarda en ir a tu casa? | How long does it take to get to your house? |
| ¿Cuánto tiempo se tarda de Bilbao a Santander? | How long does it take to get from Bilbao to Santander? |

It can also be used to express the idea of taking a long time.

He tardado porque me he encontrado con Lola	I have been a long time because I bumped into Lola
No tardes	Don't take too long
He tardado en terminarlo porque he estado mal	I have taken a long time to finish it because I have been ill

In the letter you saw an expression with the verb **tardar**:

| A más tardar | At the latest |
| Volverá el martes a más tardar | S/he will come back on Tuesday at the latest |

Según

This normally means 'according to':

| Según él, todos están locos | According to him everybody is mad |
| Según Pedro, María está enamorada | According to Pedro, María is in love |

Colloquially, however, it can be used to leave someone in suspense:

| – ¿Vienes mañana? | Are you coming tomorrow? |
| – Según | Depends |

More about letters

It is very important to know the conventions when writing a formal letter. You should write the date in the top right-hand corner of the paper.

6 de julio de 1995

Remember that the months of the year do not have capital letters.

On the left-hand side of the letter, you should write the name of the person you are sending the letter to, and/or their position in the company. This is followed by the address:

Sr. Mario López García/El Director
Gran Vía 215
Madrid

Remember that the number comes after the name of the street.

There are many ways of addressing a person in a letter, but whatever you use, you must follow it with a colon:

Estimado Señor:
Estimada Señora:
Estimada Srta. López:
Muy Sr. Mío:
Muy Sra. Mía:

The most common way of ending a formal letter is with the phrase:

Le saluda atentamente,

Pronunciation/spelling

Spanish words can be divided into three groups according to where the stress of the word is. When the last syllable of the word is stressed, a written accent is placed above the vowel of the last syllable if the word ends in a vowel or the consonants **n** or **s**.

espa*ñol*	co*lor*	ca*lor*
so*fá*	ca*fé*	be*bí*
panta*lón*	ca*mión*	bebe*rás*

Language in use

Exercise 7

You are working with a family in Madrid. You would like to visit somewhere outside Madrid on your day off. However, you don't want to spend too long on the train so you go to the railway station and ask how long the journey is to: Toledo, Alcalá de Henares, Ávila, Aranjuez and El Escorial.

Exercise 8

You have arranged to meet a friend to go to the cinema. However, you are late for no reason. Think of three reasons you could give for being late.

e.g. **He tardado porque se me ha pinchado una rueda**
I am late because I had a puncture

Exercise 9

You are supposed to have done a number of things. When your friend asks you if you have done them, say you haven't, and give a reason.

1 ¿Has llamado ya a Manolo?
2 ¿Has visto ya la película *El piano*?
3 ¿Has leído ya el libro que te dejé?
4 ¿Has hecho ya el trabajo?
5 ¿Has mandado ya la solicitud?

Exercise 10

You are staying with some Spanish friends. One of them is on the phone so you can only hear what she says. What do you think the other person says?

SUSANA: ¿Sí?
PERSONA: _____
SUSANA: Hola, Antonio, ¿qué tal?
ANTONIO: _____
SUSANA: Muy bien.
ANTONIO: _____
SUSANA: Estuve toda la noche en casa.
ANTONIO: _____
SUSANA: No, vino Luisa.
ANTONIO: _____
SUSANA: Vimos una película en la tele y después charlamos un rato.
ANTONIO: _____
SUSANA: A las doce y media, o algo así.
ANTONIO: _____
SUSANA: Vale ¿a qué hora?
ANTONIO: _____
SUSANA: De acuerdo, hasta luego.

Exercise 11

Write a similar letter to the one written by Mike Land. However, change the objects that you have bought, and the reason for needing them urgently.

Vocabulary building

Exercise 12

Here is a list of other words related to the weather. Try to match
them with their English equivalents. Before looking in the glossary,
think of the roots of some of the words as they will give you a clue
to their meaning.

1	**cielo despejado**	(a)	drizzle
2	**nubes y claros**	(b)	fog
3	**cielo cubierto**	(c)	frost
4	**chubascos**	(d)	clear sky
5	**llovizna**	(e)	storm
6	**tormenta**	(f)	cloudy
7	**heladas**	(g)	clouds with clear patches
8	**niebla**	(h)	heavy showers

Exercise 13

Here are some more expressions of time. Arrange them into three
different groups according to their references to the past, present or
future:

anteayer	esta noche
anoche	ahora
mañana a mediodía	mañana por la mañana
esta tarde	anteanoche
ahora mismo	hace unas horas

Reading

*A few weeks ago you wrote a letter for a friend who wants to go to
Spain on holiday in August. You wrote to Hotel La Colina asking
them to book a double room with sea views. The hotel has replied to
your letter. Tell your friend when the room has been booked for and
whether the room has sea views*

Hotel La Colina
Plaza San Bartolomé s/n
Tel. 4868345
Bermeo

Bermeo, 8 de julio de 1995

Sr. John Hardy
15, Colehill Lane
London, S.W. 6

Muy Señor Mío:

Acusamos recibo de su atenta carta de fecha 15 de junio y nos es grato informarle que le hemos reservado una habitación doble con cuarto de baño para una semana a partir del 15 de agosto.

Lamentamos tener que decirle que para esas fechas no tenemos disponible ninguna habitación con vista al mar.

Le saludamos muy atentamente,

Guía de Santander

Santander es la capital de la Comunidad Autónoma de Cantabria. Situada en el norte de la Península, disfruta de un clima templado, con una máxima de 25 grados en verano y 14 en invierno.

Aviaco tiene vuelos directos desde Madrid, Barcelona y Pamplona a diario. En tren hay buena comunicación con Madrid, vía Palencia, Ávila, Valladolid y Segovia.

Santander tiene una gama de alojamientos de distinta categoría, desde el hotel de lujo, a las residencias y hostales de trato familiar, muchas de ellas abiertas sólo en verano.

Santander cuenta con gran variedad de restaurantes, desde los de alta cocina a las tascas de pescado del Barrio Pesquero. Son famosos sus quesos, pescados, y mariscos.

13 Un robo

A robbery

In this lesson we will look at:
- descriptions of people
- talking about habitual past actions
- intensifying a description
- the relative pronouns **que** and **quien**
- the imperfect tense

Dialogue

At the police station

Liz, an American tourist, has been robbed whilst walking in El Barrio Gótico, in Barcelona. She goes to the police station to report the theft

POLICÍA: Buenas tardes, señorita, ¿En qué puedo ayudarle?

LIZ: Me acaban de robar todo.

POLICÍA: ¿Dónde ha sido?

LIZ: Muy cerca de aquí, en una de las calles del Barrio Gótico.

POLICÍA: ¿Vio quién le robó?

LIZ: Sí mire. Iba andando cuando dos hombres se acercaron a pedirme fuego. Iba a sacar el mechero cuando uno de ellos sacó una navaja. Se llevaron todo, el dinero, las tarjetas de crédito, la cámara y hasta la chaqueta de cuero.

POLICÍA: ¿Cómo eran?

LIZ: Sí, el de la navaja era bajo pero bastante fuerte. Llevaba el pelo muy corto. Llevaba puesta una chaqueta oscura y pantalones vaqueros. El otro era rubio, alto, y delgado. Llevaba una chaqueta de cuero negra y pantalones vaqueros del mismo color.

POLICÍA: Bien, mire, de momento tiene que rellenar esta hoja. Si deja su dirección y un número de teléfono nos pondremos en contacto con usted.

Language points

Que/quien

The pronoun **que** is often used to express the relative pronoun 'who', regardless of whether it refers to a person or a thing.

¿Viste al hombre que vive ahí? Did you see the man who lives there?

La mujer que me robó es rubia The woman who robbed me is blonde

However, when the relative pronoun has a preposition, **quien** is used after the preposition when it refers to a person; and **que** is used when it refers to things.

El hombre con quien saliste está casado The man you went out with is married

| La mujer a quien has saludado es rusa | The woman you have greeted is Russian |
| La novela de que hablas es de García Márquez | The novel you are talking about is by García Márquez |

The imperfect tense

You will probably have noticed in the dialogue that there are various past tenses. You already know the preterite and the present perfect. The other main one is the imperfect. The main uses of the imperfect tense are:

- for talking about events that used to happen
- for descriptions
- to express continuance and duration

To form the imperfect tense of **-ar** regular verbs, the following endings are added to the infinitive without the **-ar**:

Llev*aba* pantalones vaqueros	*I was wearing* jeans
¿Llev*abas* la chaqueta de cuero?	*Were you wearing* the leather jacket?
Llev*aba* una camisa azul	*S/he was wearing* a blue shirt
Llev*ábamos* sombreros	*We were wearing* hats
¿Llev*abais* las llaves?	*Were you taking* the keys?
Llev*aban* los cinturones de seguridad puestos	*They were wearing* their seatbelts

Tener

The imperfect tense of regular **-er** and **-ir** verbs is the same. To form the imperfect tense of these verbs you add the following endings to the infinitive form without the **-er** or **-ir**:

De pequeña ten*ía* pecas	When I was little *I had* freckles
¿Ten*ías* pecas?	*Did you have* freckles?
Pedro ten*ía* una hermana	Pedro *had* a sister
Ten*íamos* razón	*We were* right
¿Ten*íais* televisión?	*Did you have* a television?
Sólo ten*ían* un dormitorio	*They* only *had* one bedroom

Notice that all these endings have an accent over the **í**.

Ser

The imperfect tense of this verb is irregular:

Yo *era* muy traviesa	*I used to be* very naughty
¿*Eras* rubia de pequeña?	*Were you* blonde when you were young?
Pedro *era* moreno de pequeño	Pedro *used to be* dark when he was young
Mis hermanos y yo *éramos* muy malos	My brothers and I *were* very bad
¿*Erais* así de pequeños?	*Were you* like this when you were young?
Eran los dos muy altos	*They were* both very tall

Ir

This verb is also irregular:

Iba a una escuela mixta	*I used to go* to a mixed school
¿*Ibas* a la playa mucho?	*Did you used to go* to the beach often?
Iba a estudiar derecho	*S/he was going* to study law
Íbamos todos juntos	*We used to go* together
¿*Ibais* a esa escuela?	*Did you used to go* to that school?
Iban siempre juntos	*They* always *used to go* together

Spanish culture

There are three types of police in Spain: the **Policía Nacional**, the **Policía Municipal** and the **Guardia Civil**. In the Basque Country (Euskadi) there is also an autonomous Basque police force, **la Ertzaintza**, and in Cataluña, **los Mozos de Escuadra**. Don't be surprised to see them all armed.

Language in use

Exercise 1

Fill in the missing forms of the verbs:

	jugar	**ver**	**salir**	**vivir**	**pasar**	**leer**
Yo	jugaba			vivía		
Tú						leías
Él		veía	salía		pasaba	

Exercise 2

Answer the following questions using the imperfect tense:

1 ¿Con quién jugabas de pequeña/o?
2 ¿Dónde estudiabas cuando tenías once años?
3 ¿Dónde vivías cuando tenías ocho años?
4 ¿Veías mucho la televisión de pequeña/o?
5 ¿De pequeño/a leías mucho o poco?
6 ¿Ibas mucho al cine?

Exercise 3

If you were to meet one of your favourite Spanish actors/actresses what would you like to know about their childhood? Write down a few questions that you would ask them.

Exercise 4

Many people change from when they were little. Answer the following questions about yourself.

1 ¿Eras rubio/a o moreno/a?
2 ¿Eras alto/a o bajo/a?
3 ¿Eras delgado/a o gordito/a?
4 ¿Eras tímido/a o abierto/a?
5 ¿Eras alegre?

Exercise 5

Fill in the appropriate relative pronoun **que** or **quien**:

1 No me has dicho con _____ fuiste a la fiesta.
2 Hablé por fin con el chico _____ estaba en la fiesta.
3 No me has dicho de _____ es el coche.
4 ¿Vio al hombre _____ conducía el coche rojo?
5 El chico con _____ está bailando Lola es muy guapo.

Dialogue 🔲

An accident

Susan meets a Spanish friend whose arm is broken and in plaster

SUSAN: Pero mujer ¿qué te ha pasado?

MERCEDES: Nada que me he roto el brazo.

SUSAN: ¿Cómo ha sido?

MERCEDES: Es que tuve un accidente de coche hace un mes.

SUSAN: ¿Ah sí? Pues no sabía nada. ¿Con quién ibas?

MERCEDES: Iba con Eder. Volvíamos de la fiestas de Bilbao, íbamos muy despacio porque había niebla, cuando de repente en una curva un coche se nos vino encima. Del resto no me acuerdo.

SUSAN: Y Eder ¿qué tal está?

MERCEDES: Pues estuvo muy grave pero ahora ya está fuera de peligro.

SUSAN: ¡Qué horror! Oye, ¿se puede ir a verle?

MERCEDES: Sí claro, además le haría mucha ilusión verte. ¡No sabes lo aburrido que es estar en un hospital!

SUSAN: Vale, ¿en qué hospital está?

MERCEDES: En Cruces, pero no puedes ir sin tarjeta de visita. Antes de ir llama a su familia.

SUSAN: De acuerdo. Bueno, me tengo que ir ahora. A ver si te pones bien pronto.

MERCEDES: Gracias. Adiós.

Language points

Imperfect and preterite

The imperfect tense very often appears in the same sentence as the preterite to express that something was going on when something else happened: that is, an interrupted event.

Volvíamos de las fiestas cuando un coche se nos echó encima.
We were coming back from the fiestas when a car hit us.

Veníamos de Londres cuando ocurrió el accidente.
We were coming from London when the accident happened.

Salíamos de casa cuando llamaron a la puerta.
We were leaving the house when they knocked on the door.

Cuando me iba sonó el teléfono.
When I was leaving the telephone rang.

Ya me iba cuando llegó Luis.
I was already leaving when Luis arrived.

Había

The imperfect form of the impersonal verb **hay** is **había**. Remember that the same form is used for singular and plural subjects.

Había más de trescientas personas	There were more than 300 people
Había niebla	It was foggy
Había tres bares en el pueblo	There were three bars in the village
¿Cuántos chicos había?	How many boys were there?

Hacer ilusión

This expression is often used to means 'to be pleased' or 'to look forward'.

Me hace mucha ilusión verte	I am very pleased to see you
Le haría mucha ilusión verte	He would be very pleased to see you
Me ha hecho mucha ilusión verle	I am very pleased that I have seen him
Me hace mucha ilusión ir a París	I am looking forward to going to Paris

Lo . . . que . . .

When you want to intensify an adjective then you use the neutral article **lo** with the adjective, plus **que**. The adjective agrees with the noun you are referring to.

No sabes lo guapo que es	You can't imagine how handsome he is
No sabes lo guapa que es	You can't imagine how pretty she is

No sabes lo bonitos que son	You can't imagine how pretty they are
No sabes lo aburrido que es	You can't imagine how boring it is
Ya sabes lo buenas que son	You know how good they are

In the first example, **guapo** refers to a man and in the second **guapa** refers to a woman. In the third sentence **bonitos** could refer, for example, to some pictures (**los cuadros**), and in the last sentence **buenas** could refer, for example, to some apples (**las manzanas**).

Pronunciation/spelling ▢▢

When the stress falls on the penultimate syllable of a word, the vowel of that syllable only carries a written accent when the word ends in a consonant, with the exception of **n** and **s**.

ven*ta*na   *si*lla   lle*ga*das
a*zú*car   *ár*bol   *fá*cil

Language in use

Exercise 6

Match the sentences so that they make sense:

1 ¿Has estado en Londres alguna vez?
2 ¿Has leído *El Quijote*?
3 ¿Has probado esas piñas?
4 ¿Has visto la película *La ley del deseo*?
5 ¿Has estado en el Prado?
6 ¿Has comido alguna vez comida japonesa?

(a) No sabes lo buenas que están
(b) No sabes lo divertida que es
(c) No sabes lo grande que es
(d) No sabes lo extraña que es
(e) No sabes lo divertido que es
(f) No sabes lo interesante que es

Exercise 7

Answer the following questions:

1 ¿Había mucha gente en el último concierto que estuviste?
2 ¿Había mucha gente en el metro hoy?
3 ¿Había mucha gente en la última playa que estuviste?

Exercise 8

Choose the appropriate tense, either the imperfect or the preterite.

(estar) en la ducha cuando (oír) un ruido. (salir) de la ducha. Cuando (salir) del cuarto de baño (ver) a un hombre que justo pasaba al comedor. Pegué un grito y por unos segundos se quedó mirándome. (ser) un hombre bastante mayor, de unos cincuenta años, y (tener) el pelo completamente blanco. (llevar) gafas y no sé por qué pero estoy segura de que (tener) los ojos verdes. Se dio la vuelta y salió corriendo por la puerta que (estar) abierta. (ir) tras él pero para cuando me di cuenta ya estaba muy lejos.

Vocabulary building

Exercise 9

Here are some adjectives for describing people. Can you match them with their opposites?

alto/a	antipático/a
tranquilo/a	desagradable
simpático/a	bajo/a
guapo/a	tonto/a
agradable	nervioso/a
listo/a	feo/a

Exercise 10

You are describing your ideal man/woman to a Spanish friend. From the following list of adjectives, choose the ones you would use, and put them in order of importance.

guapo/a, alegre, simpático/a, valiente, serio/a, generoso/a, trabajador/a, atlético/a, rico/a, ambicioso/a, inteligente, amable, honesto/a, fiel

Exercise 11

Many adjectives in Spanish are formed by adding **-able**, **-ible** and **-dor** to the root of some infinitives.

e.g. **amar**   **amable**

Match the verbs with their corresponding adjectives:

desear	vencedor
temer	razonable
perder	soñador
servir	servible/útil
razonar	lavable
vencer	perdedor
soñar	temible
lavar	deseable

Reading

Here is a description of a town in the evening. Remember that Spanish people like to go out after work for a walk: el paseo. *The extract is from the novel* La Regenta *written by the Spanish writer* Clarín. *It was first published in 1885*

Cuando llegaban a las primeras casas de Vetusta, oscurecía. La luz amarillenta del gas brillaba de trecho en trecho, cerca de las ramas polvorientas de las raquíticas acacias que adornaban el boulevar, nombre popular de la calle por donde entraban en el pueblo.

Al anochecer, hora en que dejaban el trabajo los obreros, se convertía aquella acera en paseo, donde era díficil andar sin pararse a cada tres pasos. Costureras, chalequeras, planchadoras, ribeteadoras, cigarreras, fosforeras y armeros, zapateros, sastres, carpinteros y hasta albañiles y canteros, sin contar otras muchas clases de industriales, se daban cita bajo las acacias del triunfo y paseaban allí una hora, arrastrando los pies sobre las piedras con estridente sonsonete.

1 Which words help us to know that it is early evening?
2 How long did the **paseo** usually last?
3 Here are some professions, women's and men's, according to the period when it was written. Which professions do you think still exist?

fosforera	hacen cerillas
ribeteadoras	cosen zapatos
costureras	cosen ropa
chalequeras	(tailor's assistant)

14 Esperanzas para el futuro

Future hopes

In this lesson we will look at:

- talking about the future and using the future tense
- more uses of the conditional
- the verb **hacerse**

The following is an extract from a play called Historia de una escalera *by the Spanish playwright, Buero Vallejo. In this extract Fernando talks to the woman he loves about his plans for the future*

FERNANDO: Sí, acabar con todo esto. ¡Ayúdame tú! Escucha: voy a estudiar mucho, ¿sabes? Mucho. Primero me haré delineante. ¡Eso es fácil! En un año ... Como para entonces ya ganaré bastante, estudiaré para aparejador solicitado por todos los arquitectos. Ganaré mucho dinero. Por entonces tú serás ya mi mujercita, y viviremos en otro barrio, en un pisito limpio y tranquilo. Yo seguiré estudiando. ¿Quién sabe? Puede que para entonces me haga ingeniero. Y como una cosa no es incompatible con la otra, publicaré un libro de poesías, un libro que tendrá mucho éxito ...

CARMINA: (*Que le ha escuchado extasiada.*) ¡Qué felices seremos!

FERNANDO: ¡Carmina!

Language points

The future tense

You have already learned how to express future actions with **ir a**. Fernando uses it in his speech.

Voy a estudiar mucho	I am going to study a lot

However, the rest of Fernando's statements are made using the future tense. You will probably have noticed that to form the future tense you use the whole infinitive verb: **estudiar**, **ganar**, **ser**, etc. and add the following endings:

Estudia*ré* mucho	*I shall study* a lot
¿Vivir*ás* con tus padres?	*Will you live* with your parents?
Publicar*á* la novela el año que viene	*S/he will publish* the novel next year
Vivir*emos* en otro barrio	*We shall live* in another area
¿Os ir*éis* el mes que viene?	*Will you leave* next month?
Se ir*án* pasado mañana	*They will leave* the day after tomorrow

The endings are the same for **-ar**, **-er** and **-ir** regular verbs.

There are, however, some irregular verbs that do not follow the above rule. One of them appears at the end of Fernando's speech:

Un libro que *tendrá* mucho éxito	A book that *will be* a success

The verb **tener** is one of the irregular verbs whose root changes in the same way as the verbs **poner** and **venir**. However, as you can see, the endings are the same as for the other verbs.

Tendré **que ir mañana**	*I shall have* to go tomorrow
¿*Vendrás* **mañana?**	*Will you come* tomorrow?
Vendrá **pasado mañana**	*S/he will come* the day after tomorrow
Tendremos **que cocinar mucho**	*We shall have* to cook a lot
¿**Dónde lo** *pondréis*?	Where *will you* put it?
Lo *pondrán* **en el salón**	*They will put* it in the sitting room

Hacerse

Another useful irregular verb is used at the beginning of Fernando's speech:

Primero *me haré* **delineante**	First *I shall become* a draughtsman

This is from the verb **hacer**:

Haré las compras	I shall do the shopping
¿Harás eso por él?	Will you do that for him?
Lo hará si se lo pido	S/he will do it if I ask her/him

However, when the verb **hacer** is conjugated as a reflexive verb it means 'to become'. It generally means to become something after making an effort.

Se hizo médico	He became a doctor

Para entonces

In order to convey the meaning of something happening by a certain time (i.e. 'by then'), use the preposition **para** and not **por**:

Para entonces ya seré médico	By then I shall be a doctor
Para entonces ya tendrá suficiente dinero	By then s/he will have enough money

Used with the preposition **por** it means 'at that time', 'then':

Por entonces no había electricidad	At that time there was no electricity
Por entonces no había agua corriente	At that time there was no running water
Por aquel entonces no teníamos calefacción central	At that time we did not have central heating

Language in use

Exercise 1

Join the appropriate sentences together:

1 Tendré que ir a verlo porque   (a) si quieres saber la verdad
2 Tendrás que estudiar   (b) está enfermo
3 Tendré que saludarle   (c) si quieres cobrar
4 Tendrás que terminarlo   (d) si no quieres suspender
5 Tendrás que preguntarle   (e) si quiero adelgazar
6 Tendré que dejar de comer chocolate   (f) si es que le veo en la calle

Spanish culture

Once a year every village, town and city in Spain celebrates the local saint's day, the harvest . . . any excuse for a party. These fiestas can last from one day to two weeks. During the fiestas many diverse events will take place, from bicycle races to giant carnival figures which run down the streets terrorising children, but whatever there may be, there will always be lots of music, dancing, food and drink. Among some of the most famous fiestas are the **Fallas** of San José in Valencia (12–19 March) where millions of pesetas worth of carnival floats and figures are burnt during the last night of the fiesta.

San Fermín in Pamplona (7–13 July) is perhaps one of the most famous fiestas thanks to the American writer, Ernest Hemingway. The day begins with the **encierro** or running of the bulls. Before and after the daily bullfights, bands playing music, regional dancing and parades take over the streets. The **Fiestas de Santiago de Mayor** (25 July) are celebrated in Santiago de Compostela (La Coruña) for two weeks with Galician music, dance and theatre, and a livestock fair. The key event is the mass on 25 July. **El Misterio de Elche** (11–15 August) is perhaps the most famous among the many fiestas held in Spain to celebrate the Virgen de la Asunción. It has been declared a fiesta of National Tourist Interest. Amateur actors from the neighbourhood of Elche (Alicante) rehearse during the year to perform the Elche mystery play, a sacred drama from the 13th century.

Exercise 2

A Spanish friend of yours is going to visit your country. Tell her/him some of the things s/he will have to do.

   e.g. **Tendrás que levantarte**   You will have to get up early
   temprano

Exercise 3

Write four sentences using one word from each column as necessary

mis	tiendas	vendrán	Londres	las		
la	iré	empezará	a	domingo	nueve
las	fiesta	abrirán	a	mañana	doce
yo	padres	a	el	las	

Exercise 4

You are talking with a group of Spanish friends about what you are planning to do next year. Write down a few things that you think you will be doing.

e.g. **El año que viene creo que iré a Venezuela de vacaciones**

Exercise 5

If you have the cassettes, listen to them. What does Ramón hope to do next year?

Dialogue

Attending to business

Mr Hampson, a businessman from New York, is in Madrid arranging some orders. He is talking about the time of arrival of one of the orders

MR HAMPSON: ¿Cúando podrá mandar el último pedido?
SR. LOPEZ: Estará listo la semana que viene
MR HAMPSON: ¿Tardará mucho en llegar a Nueva York?
SR. LOPEZ: Mire, depende de cómo se mande; si lo mandamos por correo aéreo estará en su oficina en menos de cinco días, en cambio si lo mandamos por barco tardará unas cinco semanas.¿Le corre prisa?
MR HAMPSON: Pues sí, bastante
SR. LOPEZ: Entonces sería mejor mandarlo por avión, ¿no?
MR HAMPSON: ¿Costará mucho más?
SR. LOPEZ: Algo así como el uno por ciento del coste total.

Language points

Future tense of *poder*

As you will probably have noticed, the future tense of **poder** is irregular.

¿Cúando *podrá* mandar el pedido?	When *will you be able* to send the order?

¿Podrás **hacerlo tú solo?**	*Will you be able* to do it on your own?
Si quieres *podré* **ir el lunes**	If you want *I shall be able* to go on Monday

Si

We saw in Lesson 7 that if the conditional **si** is followed by a present tense then the verb in the main sentence must go either into the present, the imperative or the future. The last case appears in the dialogue.

Si lo mandamos por barco tardará cinco semanas	If we send it by sea it will take five weeks
Si viene pronto le recibiré	If s/he comes early I shall meet him/her

Estar listo

This expression is often used in Spanish meaning 'to be ready':

¿Estás listo?	Are you ready?
Está todo listo para el viaje	Everything is ready for the journey
¿Están listos los paquetes?	Are the parcels ready?
Las niñas ya están listas	The girls are ready

Note that as **listo** is an adjective, it takes the gender and number of the objects that it qualifies:

¿Está la tarta lista?	Is the cake ready?

When **listo** is used with the verb **ser**, it then means 'clever'.

Pedro es muy listo	Pedro is very clever

Remember that in order to talk about being in a hurry, Spanish uses the verb **tener** (to have):

¿Tienes prisa?	Are you in a hurry?

However, if something is urgent you can use the colloquial expression:

Me corre prisa	It is urgent
¿Te corre prisa?	Is it urgent?

En cambio

This expression is normally used meaning 'on the other hand':

Yo la llamo todos los días, ella en cambio me llama sólo una vez al mes
I call her every day, on the other hand she only calls me once a month

Pronunciation/spelling ⬚

All words that carry the stress on the third-to-last syllable have a written accent:

fábrica   **plá**tano   te**lé**fono   **mú**sica   **mé**dico

Language in use

Exercise 6

Match the following statements:

1 Si te levantas temprano
2 Si va contigo
3 Si estudias mucho
4 Si vas a esa fiesta
5 Si vienes conmigo

(a) verás a Pedro
(b) tendrás tiempo para todo
(c) podrás conocer a mis padres
(d) sacarás buenas notas
(e) podrá venir más tarde

Exercise 7

A friend of yours wants to know something. You do not know yet, but you will know tomorrow, or soon. Answer the following questions

   e.g.   ¿Sabes a qué hora viene Pedro?
          No, pero lo sabré mañana

1 ¿Has ido al banco?
2 ¿Has leído el artículo?
3 ¿Le has escrito a tu madre?
4 ¿Sabes a qué hora sale el avión?
5 ¿Tienes ya los billetes?
6. ¿Has hablado ya con tu hermano?

Exercise 8

You had promised to have some things ready. However, when asked for them you have to explain that they are not ready yet.

  e.g. ¿Me das los apuntes?
      Lo siento, no están listos todavía

1 ¿Me das los paquetes?
2 ¿Me das la carta?
3 ¿Me das el artículo?
4 ¿Me das el pastel?
5 ¿Me das las redacciones?

Exercise 9

An English friend of yours has received a card in Spanish from a penfriend. She wants to know what it says so she has asked you to translate it for her.

Querida Lesley:

Muchas gracias por la invitación. Llegaré al aeropuerto de Gatwick el 16 de julio a las cuatro de la tarde. Iré con una amiga que sabe inglés así que no te preocupes de ir a Gatwick. Desde la estación de Victoria cogeré un taxi. ¿Estarás en casa esa tarde?

Si hay algún problema, llámame.

Un abrazo

Vocabulary building

Exercise 10

As you have probably noticed, many opposites are made by adding the prefix **in** to the adjective. Remember that if the adjective starts with a **b** or a **p**, it becomes **im**.

  compatible   **incompatible**

Now make the opposite of the following adjectives. Look up any words that you don't know in the glossary.

posible	_____	cómodo	_____
adecuado	_____	curable	_____
capaz	_____	experto	_____
cierto	_____	feliz	_____
coherente	_____	justo	_____

When the adjective starts with an **l**, just add **i**:

legal	**ilegal**
legítimo	_____
limitado	_____
lógico	_____

Reading

In the extract at the beginning of this lesson, Fernando talks about his plans for the future. However, in the next scene we see that Fernando has married somebody else because of her money. The play ends with Fernando's son's speech to Carmina's daughter. The speech is almost identical to his father's

FERNANDO, HIJO: Sí, Carmina. Aquí sólo hay brutalidad e incomprensión para nosotros. Escúchame. Si tu cariño no me falta, emprenderé muchas cosas. Primero me haré aparejador. ¡No es difícil! En unos años me haré un buen aparejador. Ganaré mucho dinero y me solicitarán todas las empresas constructoras. Para entonces ya estaremos casados. Tendremos nuestro hogar, alegre y limpio . . . , lejos de aquí. Pero no dejaré de estudiar por eso. ¡No, no, Carmina! Entonces me haré ingeniero. Seré el mejor ingeniero del país y tú serás mi adorada mujercita . . .

CARMINA, HIJA: ¡Fernando! ¡Qué felicidad! . . . ¡Qué felicidad!

FERNANDO, HIJO: ¡Carmina!

1 What does Fernando's son need to fulfil his dreams?
2 What is the difference between Fernando's and his son's first jobs?
3 What does Fernando want to do that his son does not mention?

15 Una invitación

An invitation

In this lesson we will look at:

- expressing hope
- denying a belief
- asking people to do things for you
- the verbs **ponerse**, **acordarse** and **dejar**
- the present subjunctive

Dialogue 🔲

Confirming an invitation

Liz has been living in Valencia with her boyfriend for a few months. They have been invited to dinner at the home of Asun, Liz's Spanish teacher. Liz phones her to check the time they have to be there, and to excuse Mark, a friend of theirs, who is not feeling too well

ASUN: ¿Sí, dígame?

LIZ: Asun, soy Liz. Mira, no me acuerdo a qué hora quieres que estemows en tu casa.

ASUN: Hacia las nueve. Lewis y Mark vienen contigo ¿no?

LIZ: Lewis viene seguro pero no creo que venga Mark, no se encuentra muy bien

ASUN: Ah, cuánto lo siento. Espero que se ponga bueno para mañana, porque se va mañana ¿no?

LIZ: Sí, por cierto, si quieres venir mañana a casa a despedirte . . .

ASUN: Muy buena idea. ¿A qué hora se va?

LIZ: Creo que a las cuatro de la tarde.

ASUN: Bien, luego hablamos. Hasta luego.
LIZ: Hasta luego.

Language points

The subjunctive

You may have heard this word with horror since it refers to a mood that is seldom used in English: 'if I were a rich man' is an example. Do not worry! The best way to learn how to use it is by knowing that the word 'subjunctive' implies subjectivity. Therefore, whenever there is a possibility that the action you are referring to may not take place, you use the subjunctive. This is why it is very often found when there is a change of subject in the sentence, and with certain expressions that have an element of subjectivity such as **es probable** ('it is probable').

There is not time to learn all about the subjunctive in this course, but it's useful to have an idea about some of its uses.

You have learned how to express a wish:

Quiero trabajar aquí	I want to work here
Quiero estudiar derecho	I want to study law

However, when you want someone else to do something there is always a doubt that the person will do it. In order to express that doubt, Spanish uses the subjunctive form:

Quiero que *trabajes* **aquí**	I want *you to work* here
Quiero que *estudies* **derecho**	I want *you to study* law

The present subjunctive for **-ar** verbs is formed by adding the following endings to the present indicative. Take the first person, **trabajo**, drop the **o** and add the following endings:

Él quiere que yo trabaje más	He wants me *to work* more
Él quiere que trabajes más	He wants you *to work* more
Yo quiero que trabaje más	I want him/her *to work* more
¿Quieres que trabajemos más?	Do you want us *to work* more?
Él quiere que trabajéis más	He wants you *to work* more
Quiero que trabajen más	I want them *to work* more

Note that the first person of the present subjunctive has no accent, which distinguishes it from the preterite **trabajé** (I worked).

The **-er** and **-ir** regular verbs have the following endings:

¿Quieres que com*a* en tu casa?	Do you want me *to eat* at your house?
Quiero que com*as* todo	I want you *to eat* everything
Quiero que com*a* todo	I want him/her *to eat* everything
¿Dónde quieres que com*amos*?	Where do you want us *to eat*?
Quiero que com*áis* en casa	I want you *to eat* at home
Quiero que com*an* aquí	I want them *to eat* here

Remember to take the first person of the present indicative, and then drop the final **o** before you add the subjunctive endings.

¿A qué hora quieres que *venga*?	At what time do you want me *to come*?
Quiero que *vengas* pronto	I want you *to come* soon

Two common verbs which do not follow any of the above patterns have appeared in the dialogue: **ir** and **estar**.

Él quiere que vaya a la universidad	He wants me *to go* to university
Quiero que vayas a la oficina	I want you *to go* to the office
Quiere que esté aquí	He wants me *to be* here
Quiero que estés aquí	I want you *to be* here

We can, therefore, say that verbs of wishing, wanting, requesting, etc., take the present subjunctive when there is a change of subject.

Te pido que vengas por favor	I am asking you to come, please
Dile que venga más tarde	Tell him to come later

In these examples, there is a chance that they may not come.

You have seen another use of the subjunctive form in the dialogue, when Liz says she does not believe that Mark will come to dinner:

No creo que venga	I don't think he will come

However, when the verb **creer** is used in the affirmative, the indicative mood is used, and not the subjunctive:

Creo que viene más tarde	I think s/he is coming later

The subjunctive is also used after the verb **esperar** (to hope) when the subject of both phrases is different.

Espero ir mañana	I hope to go tomorrow
Espero que vaya mañana	*I* hope *s/he* goes tomorrow

Ponerse

You have seen the verb **poner** meaning 'to place', 'to put':

¿Dónde pongo la tele?	Where do I put the TV?

When **poner** is used as a reflexive verb, it means 'to get better', 'to recover', or 'to fall ill', and 'to put on clothing':

Se ha puesto enferma	She has fallen ill
Se ha puesto bueno	He has recovered
Espero que te pongas bien	I hope you recover soon
Ya se ha puesto la corbata	He has already put his tie on
Se ha puesto un jersey	She has put a jumper on

Acordarse de

This reflexive verb has the same meaning as **recordar** (to remember), and both can be used interchangeably:

No me acuerdo	I don't remember
No recuerdo	I don't remember

When you want to specify what you cannot remember, then **acordarse** is followed by the preposition **de**:

No me acuerdo de su nombre	I cannot remember his/her name
No recuerdo su nombre	I cannot remember his/her name
¿Te acuerdas del título?	Do you remember the title?
Acuérdate de ir	Remember to go
Acuérdate de llamarle	Remember to call him

Language in use

Exercise 1

Find the odd one out in each line:

recibas	escribas	vengas	trabajas
pienso	duermo	creo	me parece
cierto	seguro	probable	indudable
necesario	preciso	raro	conveniente

Spanish culture
Renting a car

Most main towns have car rental firms (**empresas de alquiler de coches**). In order to rent a car you must show a full address, a telephone number and passport or identity card number. Then you will have to show your driving licence. Some firms require that the driver has three years' experience, and nearly all of them demand that the driver should be at least 21 years old. Some of them require the driver to be at least 25 years old. Prices do not vary greatly, a medium price would be about 25 euros per day plus 1 euro per kilometre, and 10 for insurance which normally only covers third party insurance (**seguro para terceros**). If you wanted to have fully comprehensive insurance (**seguro a todo riesgo**) you would have to pay a supplement of between 5 and 10 euros. Some firms let the client opt for unlimited mileage from the third day (**kilometraje ilimitado**). This costs about 40 euros per day.

Exercise 2

A Spanish friend of yours is saying things you do not agree with. Contradict what she is saying:

e.g. Creo que viene luego   No creo que venga hoy

1 Creo que está estudiando
2 Creo que está en casa
3 Creo que va mañana
4 Creo que vive en esa casa
5 Creo que trabaja en la embajada
6 Creo que sale con Dolores

Exercise 3

You are not feeling too well, so a Spanish friend offers to help out. You want him to call your office, to call the doctor, to buy some fruit and to cook an omelette.

e.g. Quiero que compres el periódico

Exercise 4

You are helping a Spanish friend to move house. You will be carrying **la televisión**, **los discos**, **los libros** and **el ordenador**. Ask her where she wants you to put them.

  e.g. ¿Dónde quieres que ponga la impresora?

Exercise 5

Here is a list of things you hope to do. You hope a friend of yours will do them as well. How would you tell him/her?

  e.g. Espero ir a Londres   Espero que vayas a Londres

1 Espero aprobar los exámenes de español
2 Espero ver a Lourdes
3 Espero aprender a conducir
4 Espero comprar un coche pronto
5 Espero encontrar una casa pronto
6 Espero venir de nuevo

Exercise 6

You and a Spanish friend are going on holiday together. Your friend keeps on forgetting to do things, such as buying the ticket, phoning her mother, booking the hotel, paying the telephone bill, buying her swimming costume (**traje de baño**). Remind her to do these things.

  e.g. Acuérdate de comprar la crema de sol

Dialogue

Asking a favour

Margaret works for a Spanish family as an au pair. The woman she works for phones her to ask her to do certain things, as she will not be coming home until late

SEÑORA: En cuanto llegues quiero que prepares la merienda para Luisito y su amigo Jaime. Después de merendar no quiero que vean la tele, diles que hagan los deberes primero.

MARGARET: Sí señora.
SEÑORA: Cuando terminen los deberes pueden jugar un rato en la habitación pero no les dejes jugar en el salón.
MARGARET: ¿Quiere que les prepare yo la cena?
SEÑORA: Si no te importa, por favor. Hay unos filetes de pescado en la nevera pero no creo que haya ninguna verdura fresca, así que saca algo del congelador.
MARGARET: Sí señora, no se preocupe.
SEÑORA: ¡Ah! cuando se marche Jaime mándale a Luisito que se acueste enseguida y que no me espere que voy a llegar tarde.
MARGARET: Sí señora.

Language points

Cuando/en cuanto

You may have noticed that the subjunctive has been used after the conjunctions **cuando** and **en cuanto**. These conjunctions are followed by the subjunctive when something that is said has not been experienced by the speaker. That is to say, the event will happen in the future:

Cuando llegues a casa llámale When you get home, call him
Cuando termine de estudiar iré al cine When I finish studying I will go to the cinema
Cuando vengas a Madrid iremos a El Prado When you come to Madrid we will go to the Prado Museum

These examples contrast with the use of the indicative. When the indicative mood is used, whatever is expressed by the speaker has already been experienced.

Cuando llego a casa siempre le llamo When I arrive home I always call him
Cuando termino de estudiar como I (always) eat when I finish studying
Cuando voy a Madrid siempre voy a El Prado When I go to Madrid I always go to the Prado

In these three sentences by using the indicative mood the speaker implies what normally happens, because it has happened before.

As we have seen earlier in this lesson the subjunctive is used for requests. Therefore, the subjunctive is used when you ask someone to tell another person something.

Dile que venga a las dos	Tell him to come at two o'clock
Diles que no fumen tanto	Tell them not to smoke so much
Dile que lo deje en la cocina	Tell him to leave it in the kitchen
Mándale que se acueste	Order him to go to bed

The present subjunctive of **hay** is **haya**.

No creo que haya mucha gente	I don't think there will be many people
No creo que haya problemas	I don't think there will be any problems

Remember that imperatives in their negative form take the subjunctive.

No fumes tanto	Don't smoke so much
No vuelvas muy tarde	Don't come back very late
No les dejes jugar en el salón	Don't let them play in the sitting-room

Dejar

This verb can have many meanings. A common one is 'to borrow'.

¿Me dejas un boli?	Can I borrow a pen?
¿Me dejas el coche?	Can I borrow the car?

It can also mean 'to let' and 'to allow':

No me deja fumar	S/he doesn't allow me to smoke
¿Me dejas ir con Luis?	Am I allowed to go with Luis?
No la deja salir	S/he won't let her go out

Another very common use is in imperatives asking somebody not to disturb.

¡Déjame!	Leave me!
¡Déjame en paz!	Leave me in peace!

Pronunciation/spelling

Although single-syllable words do not normally have written accents, there are some exceptions. Some single-syllable words carry an accent in order to differentiate them from other words that have the same spelling.

el niño está enfermo   él es mi padre
¿es tu padre?   tú estás loco
quiero más   quiero ir mas (pero) no puedo
mi padre compró esa casa
   para mí
¿te gusta el té?

Language in use

Exercise 7

You are planning to have a big party, so you ask a Spanish friend who is going to see some of your friends that evening to tell the others what time to come and what to bring to the party. Write down six things you would like them to do or bring.

e.g. Dile a Juan que traiga los discos de Miles Davis

Exercise 8

From the list below tick those things you would ask a friend to do if s/he were to stay in your house whilst you were on holiday.

1 Cuando salgas apaga todas las luces
2 Cuando te levantes da de comer al gato
3 Cuando salgas a la tienda deja la puerta abierta
4 Cuando vayas a dormir apaga la televisión
5 Cuando llegue el recibo de teléfono, págalo por favor
6 Cuando llamen por teléfono no contestes

Exercise 9

You arrive at a friend's house in Spain with another English person. Your Spanish friend is on holiday so you are staying in her house. There is a note from her on the table. Translate it for the benefit of your English friend who does not speak Spanish.

Querido Calos

¡Bienvenido a Llanes! Espero que os lo paséis muy bien
y que haga buen tiempo para que podáis ir a
la playa. ¡Ya sé cuánto te gusta! Cuando llegues
vete a casa de los vecinos (la que tiene un
balcón lleno de flores) y diles que ya estás
aquí. Ya saben que venías. Por favor, cuando
salgáis de la casa por la noche cerrad todas
las ventanas bien (ha habido muchos robos en
la zona últimamente).

Bueno, os veo el 15 de agosto.

Exercise 10

You are talking to a Spanish friend about things you were not
allowed to do when you were younger. Write about a few things you
were not allowed to do.

e.g.   Mi madre no me dejaba beber vino

Vocabulary building

You will have noticed that many adjectives come from the participle
form of the verb. Most of these adjectives take the verb **estar**.

cansarse   cansado

Make the adjectives that derive from the following reflexive verbs:

acostarse
levantarse
despertarse   despierto
dormirse
sentarse
vestirse
peinarse
preocuparse

Reading

Rafael Alberti, one of the greatest Spanish poets of this century, wrote the following poem in 1925. In it, you will see the use of both the subjunctive and the indicative forms after the verb **querer**

> No quiero, no, que te rías,
> ni que te pintes de azul los ojos,
> ni que te empolves de arroz la cara,
> ni que te pongas la blusa verde,
> ni que te pongas la falda grana.
> Que quiero verte muy seria,
> que quiero verte siempre muy pálida,
> que quiero verte siempre llorando,
> que quiero verte siempre enlutada.

Do you think you could write a similar poem? You will have to use some opposites. For example, Alberti uses the opposite of **reír** (to laugh): **llorar** (to cry).

Ready-reference grammar

Nouns

Nouns in Spanish are either masculine or feminine. Most nouns which end in **o** are masculine (the most common exceptions are **la mano, la radio**), and those which end in **a** are feminine (the most common exceptions are **el día, el problema, el programa**). Those nouns which end in **-ción, -sión**, and **-dad** and most nouns which end in **-ma** are feminine. Some nouns which end in **-e** are masculine while others are feminine (**el coche, la calle**).

In order to form the plural of nouns ending in **-o** and **-a** you simply add **s** (**el médico, los médicos**). For nouns which end in a consonant, **-es** is added (**el hospital, los hospitales; la canción, las canciones**). Nouns ending in **-ción** and **-sión** drop the written accent in the plural. Some nouns which end in **s** do not change in the plural (**el lunes, los lunes**).

Articles

All articles must agree with the gender and number of the noun (**el coche, los coches**).

Definite articles

	masculine	*feminine*
singular	el	la
plural	los	las

These articles are used when the speaker knows the identity of the person or object mentioned.

> ¿Dónde está el coche?

Definite articles are used with all general nouns.

> **Los gatos son independientes** Cats are independent

They are also used with days of the week, with parts of the body, and with the time.

El lunes voy al cine	I go to the cinema on Monday
¿Te has lavado las manos?	Have you washed your hands?
Me voy a las cuatro	I am leaving at four

The article **el** is contracted with the prepositions **a** and **de** to form one word.

¿Vamos al cine?	Shall we go to the cinema?
Vienen del mercado	They are coming from the market

Indefinite articles

	masculine	feminine
singular	un	una
plural	unos	unas

Indefinite articles are used when the speaker does not specify the person or object.

Ahora trabajo en un restaurante	Now I work in a restaurant

Note that the indefinite article is omitted after the verb **ser** with professions.

Él es médico	He is a doctor

The indefinite article is not used with the words **otro/a** and **medio**.

¿Tienes otra bolsa?	Do you have another bag?

Prepositions

The most frequently used Spanish prepositions are: **a**, **bajo**, **con**, **contra**, **de**, **desde**, **durante**, **en**, **entre**, **incluso**, **no obstante**, **hacia**, **hasta**, **para**, **por**, **según**, **sin**, **sobre**, **tras**. **Ante**, **sobre**, **bajo** and **tras** are normally substituted by the adverbs **delante de**, **debajo de**, **encima de**, **detrás de**:

ante	delante de	in front of
sobre	encima de	on
bajo	debajo de	under
tras	detrás de	behind

The preposition **a** is most frequently used to express direction and to form an indirect object, and a direct object when it refers to a person, not an object.

Veo a Luis todos los días	I see Luis every day
Estoy viendo una película	I am watching a film
Le di a Juan un libro	I gave Juan a book
Voy a la piscina	I am going to the swimming pool

The prepostion **a** plus the masculine article **el** becomes **al**. It is used to express distance:

Está a quince kilómetros	It is fifteen kilometres from here

It is also used to talk about time:

a las doce	at twelve o'clock

As the preposition **a** expresses direction, it should not be used with verbs that do not denote direction or movement.

Estoy en la estación	I am at the station

The preposition **en** is used to denote 'inside':

Estoy en casa	I am at home

It is also used in expressions of time:

Voy de vacaciones en agosto	I am going on holiday in August
Nací en 1958	I was born in 1958

The preposition **de** is most frequently used to express origin and possession

Soy *de* **Bilbao**	I am *from* Bilbao
El hermano *de* **Lola**	Lola*'s* brother

The preposition **de** plus the masculine article **el** becomes **del**:

Vengo *del* **cine**	I am coming *from* the cinema

desde . . . hasta/de . . . a

Voy en coche *desde* Madrid *hasta* Bilbao
Voy en coche *de* Madrid *a* Bilbao

I am going *from* Madrid *to* Bilbao by car

You can use either: **desde . . . hasta**, or **de . . . a**

por/para

Generally speaking, **para** indicates destination and intention:

Este paquete es *para* Rosa — This packet is *for* Rosa
Estudia *para* médico — He is studying to be (*in order to* become) a doctor
Se va *para* Madrid — He is leaving *for* Madrid

Para is also used to express time limit:

Lo necesito *para* el domingo — I need it *by* Sunday

Por is normally used to express the reason for an action:

Lo hago *por* él — I am doing it *for* him (*for* his sake)

This contrasts with:

Lo hago *para* él — I am doing it for him (he will receive it)

Por is also used to express an indefinite time or place:

Estaré allí *por* enero — I will be there around January
¿Hay una farmacia *por* aquí? — Is there a chemist's around here?

Adjectives

Adjectives agree with the gender and number of the noun they describe. If the adjective ends in **-o** change it to **-a** when it modifies a feminine noun.

El mercado moderno — **los mercados modernos**
La casa moderna — **las casas modernas**

Those adjectives which end in **-e** do not change with gender.

However, they agree with the number:

El chico es inteligente   **los chicos son inteligentes**
La chica es inteligente   **las chicas son inteligentes**

Most adjectives that end in a consonant do not change either. The ending **-es** is added to the adjective when the noun it qualifies is plural.

Ese hombre es popular   **esos hombres son populares**
Esa mujer es popular   **esas mujeres son populares**

Note that descriptive adjectives follow the noun.

Conchi es una chica alta   Conchi is a tall girl

However, there are some instances in which the adjective goes before the noun. The meaning in these instances changes:

Andrés tiene un coche nuevo Andrés has brand new car
Andrés tiene un nuevo coche Andrés has another car
José es un hombre pobre   José is a poor man (*no money*)
José es un pobre hombre   José is a poor man (*no luck*)

Comparision of adjectives

superiority	más *adjective* que
equality	tan *adjective* como
inferiority	menos *adjective* que

Mi coche es más grande que My car is bigger than yours
   el tuyo

Some adjectives have irregular comparative forms:

bueno	**mejor**
malo	**peor**
grande (size)	**mayor/más grande**
pequeño (size)	**menor/más pequeño**
grande (age)	**mayor**
pequeño (age)	**menor**

Possessive adjectives

Possessive adjectives agree with the gender and number of the possessed object not the gender of the person speaking.

Masculine		Feminine	
singular	plural	singular	plural
mi	mis	mi	mis
tu	tus	tu	tus
su	sus	su	sus
nuestro	nuestros	nuestra	nuestras
vuestro	vuestros	vuestra	vuestras
su	sus	su	sus

Mis hermanos viven en Vitoria	My brothers live in Vitoria
¿Dónde está vuestra casa?	Where is your house?

Masculine		Feminine	
singular	plural	singular	plural
mío	míos	mía	mías
tuyo	tuyos	tuya	tuyas
suyo	suyos	suya	suyas
nuestro	nuestros	nuestra	nuestras
vuestro	vuestros	vuestra	vuestras
suyo	suyos	suya	suyas

These adjectives can go after a noun:

Una amiga mía	A friend of mine

After a verb:

Este paraguas es tuyo ¿no?	This umbrella is yours, isn't it?

Or after an article:

Mi coche está muy viejo	My car is very old
El mío también	Mine too

Demonstrative adjectives

These adjectives agree with the gender and number of the noun they refer to.

Este/esta/estos/estas are used when the object is near the speaker.

Ese/esa/esos/esas are used when the object is near the person spoken to, but not the speaker.

Aquel/aquella/aquellos/aquellas are used when the speaker and the person spoken to are both far from the object.

Masculine		Feminine	
singular	plural	singular	plural
este	estos	esta	estas
ese	esos	esa	esas
aquel	aquellos	aquella	aquellas

Pronouns

Normally the subject pronoun is not used, as the subject is indicated by the verb ending. They are, however, used to emphasize the subject.

	First person	*Second person*	*Third person*
singular	yo	tú	él
		usted	ella
plural	nosotros	vosotros	ellos
	nosotras	vosotras	ellas
		ustedes	

Preposition plus a personal subject

	First person	*Second person*	*Third person*
singular	mí	ti	él
		usted	ella
plural	nosotros	vosotros	ellos
	nosotras	vosotras	ellas
		ustedes	

When the first and second person subjects are preceded by the preposition **con**, the following forms are used:

¿Vienes conmigo?	Are you coming with me?
Voy contigo	I am going with you

The **tú** form is used for informal address, whilst **usted** is the formal form of address.

Direct object pronouns			
	First person	*Second person*	*Third person*
singular	me	te	lo/le
			la
plural	nos	os	los/les
			las

Direct object pronouns can refer to either persons or things, and they normally precede the conjugated form of the verb.

¿Dónde has comprado esa mesa?	Where did you buy that table?
La compré en 'El Corte Inglés'	I bought it in 'El Corte Inglés'

However, the pronoun always appears after the verb in the imperative form.

Cómpralo	Buy it
Léelo	Read it

With infinitives and gerunds the pronoun can go before or after the verb:

Voy a comprarlo	I am going to buy it
Lo voy a comprar	I am going to buy it
Estoy mirándolas	I am looking at them
Las estoy mirando	I am looking at them

Indirect object pronouns			
	First person	*Second person*	*Third person*
singular	me	te	le/se
plural	nos	os	les/se

The indirect object pronouns **le/les** both change to **se** when used with the direct object pronouns **lo/los/la/las**:

Te lo di ayer	I gave it to you yesterday
Se lo di ayer	I gave it to him/her yesterday

When both the indirect and direct object pronouns appear in the same sentence, the indirect object pronoun always precedes the direct object pronoun.

Reflexive pronouns

	First person	*Second person*	*Third person*
singular	me	te	se
		se	
plural	nos	os	se
		se	

The reflexive pronoun **se** is used in the second person when the formal form of address is used.

Demonstrative pronouns

Masculine		*Feminine*	
singular	plural	singular	plural
éste	éstos	ésta	éstas
ése	ésos	ésa	ésas
aquél	aquéllos	aquélla	aquéllas

Note that these pronouns carry an accent, whilst the demonstrative adjectives do not.

Interrogatives

The most common interrogative words are the following:

¿Qué?	What?
¿Dónde?	Where?

¿Adónde?	To where?
¿Cuándo?	When?
¿Cómo?	How?
¿Quién? ¿Quiénes?	Who?
¿A quién? ¿A quiénes?	To whom?
¿Por qué?	Why?

Note that they all have a written accent.

These interrogatives do not normally cause any problems as they are very close to their English equivalents. However, many English-speaking people have difficulty in distinguishing between **¿Cúal?** and **¿Qué?** ¿Cuál? normally means 'which', or 'which one'.

 ¿Cuál prefieres?   Which one do you prefer?

There are, however, some instances where it is translated by 'what', normally when it is used with the verb **ser**.

 ¿Cuál es la capital de México? What is the capital of Mexico?

Verbs

There are three groups of verbs in Spanish. The infinitive can end in **-ar**, **-er** or **-ir**.

Present tense of regular verbs

	habl*ar*	beb*er*	viv*ir*
(yo)	habl*o*	beb*o*	viv*o*
(tú)	habl*as*	beb*es*	viv*es*
(él/ella/usted)	habl*a*	beb*e*	viv*e*
(nosotros/nosotras)	habl*amos*	beb*emos*	viv*imos*
(vosotros/vosotras)	habl*áis*	beb*éis*	viv*ís*
(ellos/ellas/ustedes)	habl*an*	beb*en*	viv*en*

Although **usted** and **ustedes** refer to the second person, they use the third person form.

Irregular verbs

	ser	*estar*	*ir*
(yo)	soy	estoy	voy
(tú)	eres	estás	vas
(él/ella/usted)	es	está	va
(nosotros/nosotras)	somos	estamos	vamos
(vosotros/vosotras)	sois	estáis	vais
(ellos/ellas/ustedes)	son	están	van

Some irregular verbs only change in the first person singular (yo).

	poner	*hacer*	*salir*	*traer*
(yo)	pongo	hago	salgo	traigo
(tú)	pones	haces	sales	traes
(él/ella/usted)	pone	hace	sale	trae
(nosotros/nosotras)	ponemos	hacemos	salimos	traemos
(vosotros/vosotras)	ponéis	hacéis	salís	traéis
(ellos/ellas/ustedes)	ponen	hacen	salen	traen

Some verbs have double irregularity:

	venir	*tener*	*decir*	*oír*
(yo)	vengo	tengo	digo	oigo
(tú)	vienes	tienes	dices	oyes
(él/ella/usted)	viene	tiene	dice	oye
(nosotros/nosotras)	venimos	tenemos	decimos	oímos
(vosotros/vosotras)	venís	tenéis	decís	oís
(ellos/ellas/ustedes)	vienen	tienen	dicen	oyen

Some irregular verbs change the stem of the infinitive **e** to **ie**, **o** to **ue** or **u** to **ue** in all forms except **nosotros** and **vosotros**.

	querer	*poder*	*pensar*	*jugar*
(yo)	quiero	puedo	pienso	juego
(tú)	quieres	puedes	piensas	juegas
(él/ella/usted)	quiere	puede	piensa	juega
(nosotros/nosotras)	queremos	podemos	pensamos	jugamos
(vosotros/vosotras)	queréis	podéis	pensáis	jugáis
(ellos/ellas/ustedes)	quieren	pueden	piensan	juegan

Most verbs that end in **-cer** and **-cir** are also irregular in the first person singular.

	conocer	*conducir*
(yo)	conozco	conduzco
(tú)	conoces	conduces
(él/ella/usted)	conoce	conduce
(nosotros/nosotras)	conocemos	conducimos
(vosotros/vosotras)	conocéis	conducís
(ellos/ellas/ustedes)	concocen	conducen

Reflexive verbs

As the subject receives and carries out the action, reflexive verbs need an additional pronoun: **me**, **te**, **se**, **nos**, **os**, **se**.

levantarse	**llamarse**	**ducharse**
me levanto	me llamo	me ducho
te levantas	te llamas	te duchas
se levanta	se llama	se ducha
nos levantamos	nos llamamos	nos duchamos
os levantáis	os llamáis	os ducháis
se levantan	se llaman	se duchan

Present perfect

The present perfect is formed by using the present tense of the verb **haber** with the past participle of the verb that is conjugated.

	hablar	**comer**	**vivir**
he	hablado	comido	vivido
has	"	"	"
ha	"	"	"
hemos	"	"	"
habéis	"	"	"
han	"	"	"

The past participle is formed by dropping the infinitive ending and adding **-ado** to **-ar** verbs, and **-ido** to **-er** and **-ir** verbs. However, there are some verbs that have an irregular participle.

ver	*visto*	*hacer*	*hecho*
volver	vuelto	escribir	escrito
morir	muerto	poner	puesto
abrir	abierto	romper	roto
decir	dicho	descubrir	descubierto

This tense is used to express a past action that relates closely to the present. It is used with expressions such as **hoy**, **esta mañana**, **hace un rato**, etc. It is also used to express a past action without reference to a particular time.

Hemos estado en París muchas veces   We have been to Paris many times

Preterite tense

The preterite is used to express an action completed at a definite time in the past. It is used with expressions of time.

Regular verbs

	hablar	*beber*	*vivir*
(yo)	hablé	bebí	viví
(tú)	hablaste	bebiste	viviste
(él/ella/usted)	habló	bebió	vivió
(nosotros/nosotras)	hablamos	bebimos	vivimos
(vosotros/vosotras)	hablasteis	bebisteis	vivisteis
(ellos/ellas/ustedes)	hablaron	bebieron	vivieron

Irregular verbs

The verbs **ir** and **ser** have the same forms. The verb **dar** is irregular, as it is conjugated using **-er** or **-ir** regular verb endings.

ir/ser	*dar*
fui	di
fuiste	diste
fue	dio
fuimos	dimos
fuisteis	disteis
fueron	dieron

Some irregular verbs can be grouped together

infinitive	*root*	*endings*
estar	estuv–	–e
tener	tuv–	–iste
andar	anduv–	–o
poder	pud–	–imos
saber	sup–	–isteis
poner	pus–	–ieron
venir	vin–	
hacer	hic–	
querer	quis–	

The verbs **decir**, **traer** and **traducir** have a **j** in the preterite:

decir	*traer*	*traducir*
dije	traje	traduje
dijiste	trajiste	tradujiste
dijo	trajo	tradujo
dijimos	trajimos	tradujimos
dijisteis	trajisteis	tradujisteis
dijeron	trajeron	tradujeron

The verbs **leer** and **oír** take a **y** in the third person singular and plural:

leer	oír
leí	oí
leíste	oíste
leyó	oyó
leímos	oímos
leísteis	oísteis
leyeron	oyeron

Verbs like **pedir**, **repetir** and **despedir** have an **i** in the third person singular and plural:

pedir	repetir	despedirse
pedí	repetí	me despedí
pediste	repetiste	te despediste
pidió	repitió	se despidió
pedimos	repetimos	nos despedimos
pedisteis	repetisteis	os despedisteis
pidieron	repitieron	se despidieron

Imperfect tense

The imperfect tense is used to express habitual actions, continuance, and to describe in the past. The imperfect is used with adverbial expressions such as **siempre**, **de vez en cuando**, **todos los días**, etc.

Regular verbs

hablar	beber	vivir
hablaba	bebía	vivía
hablabas	bebías	vivías
hablaba	bebía	vivía
hablábamos	bebíamos	vivíamos
hablabais	bebíais	vivíais
hablaban	bebían	vivían

Irregular verbs

There are only three irregular verbs in the imperfect tense: **ir**, **ser** and **ver**.

ir	*ser*	*ver*
iba	era	veía
ibas	eras	veías
iba	era	veía
íbamos	éramos	veíamos
ibais	erais	veíais
iban	eran	veían

Future tense

All regular verbs have the same endings in the future tense. The future tense is used in the same way as it is in English.

hablar	*beber*	*vivir*
hablaré	beberé	viviré
hablarás	beberás	vivirás
hablará	beberá	vivirá
hablaremos	beberemos	viviremos
hablaréis	beberéis	viviréis
hablarán	beberán	vivirán

Some common irregular verbs in the future tense:

decir		*decir*	*tener*
querer	querré	diré	tendré
hacer	haré	dirás	tendrás
poner	pondré	dirá	tendrá
valer	valdré	diremos	tendremos
tener	tendré	direis	tendreis
salir	saldré	dirán	tendrán
venir	vendré		
caber	cabré		
poder	podré		
saber	sabré		

decir — diré

Conditional

All regular verbs have the same endings in the conditional. The conditional is used in the same way as in English.

hablar	beber	vivir
hablar*ía*	beber*ía*	vivir*ía*
hablar*ías*	beber*ías*	vivir*ías*
hablar*ía*	beber*ía*	vivir*ía*
hablar*íamos*	beber*íamos*	vivir*íamos*
hablar*íais*	beber*íais*	vivir*íais*
hablar*ían*	beber*ían*	vivir*ían*

The same verbs that are irregular in the future are irregular in the conditional.

decir	diría	*decir*
querer	querría	diría
hacer	haría	dirías
poner	pondría	diría
valer	valdría	diríamos
tener	tendría	diríais
salir	saldría	dirían
venir	vendría	
caber	cabría	
poder	podría	
saber	sabría	

The imperative

The imperative changes according to whether it is a negative, affirmative, formal or informal form of address.

The affirmative imperative			
	-ar	*-er*	*-ir*
tú	trabaja	come	abre
usted	trabaje	coma	abra
vosotros	trabajad	comed	abrid
ustedes	trabajen	coman	abran

The negative imperative			
	-ar	*-er*	*-ir*
tú	trabajes	comas	abras
usted	trabaje	coma	abra
vosotros	trabajéis	comáis	abráis
ustedes	trabajen	coman	abran

The subjunctive

As the present subjunctive is used to express what you wish to happen but may not happen, there has to be a change of subject between the main clauses.

Quiero que **vengas**   *I* want *you* to come

To form the present subjunctive of regular verbs, the ending **-o** of the first person singular of the present indicative is dropped. To this root the endings of the subjunctive are added.

hablar	*beber*	*vivir*
habl*e*	beb*a*	viv*a*
habl*es*	beb*as*	viv*as*
habl*e*	beb*a*	viv*a*
habl*emos*	beb*amos*	viv*amos*
habl*éis*	beb*áis*	viv*áis*
habl*en*	beb*an*	viv*an*

Note that these endings are the reverse of those used for the indicative.

Ser and *estar*

Ser

This verb is used for:

nationalities	**Soy de Australia**
identity	**¿Eres el hermano de Carmen?**
professions	**Soy profesora**

description of people/places /objects	**Madrid es bastante grande**
the time	**Son las dos**
possession	**¿Es este libro tuyo?**

Estar

This verb is used for:

location	**El museo está en el centro**
description of situations	**Pedro está comiendo**
physical state	**Estoy cansado**

Some words change their meaning when used with **ser** or **estar**:

	ser	*estar*
listo	clever	ready
aburrido	boring	bored
divertido	amusing	amused
enfermo	sickly	sick

Hay/está(n)

The impersonal form of the verb **haber** is used to express the existence of something that is unknown.

¿Hay una farmacia por aquí cerca?

Está/están are used to express the existence of people or things that we know exist.

¿Dónde está el museo de El Prado?

Gustar/parecer/doler

These verbs are always used with the indirect object. The subject of these verbs normally comes at the end of the sentence.

Me duele la cabeza
Les gusta los mariscos
¿Te gustan esas botas?

Note that these verbs have only two endings: a singular and a plural form.

Adverbs

Adverbs of denial, doubt and afffirmation

también	also	**tampoco**	neither
sí	yes	**no**	no
tal vez	maybe	**quizás**	perhaps

También/tampoco

When you agree with something another person has said, **también** is used with affirmative sentences, and **tampoco** with negative ones:

Vivo en el centro No tengo televisión
Yo también   Yo tampoco

Adverbs of quantity

bastante	enough	**poco**	little
mucho	much	**nada**	nothing
demasiado	too much	**muy**	very
más	more	**menos**	less

Muy/mucho

Muy is followed by an adjective or an adverb:

Ese coche es muy rápido
Estoy muy bien

Mucho is followed by a noun:

Hay muchos restaurantes

It is also used after a verb:

Trabaja mucho

Algo/nada; alguien/nadie

Has comprado algo?
No he comprado nada

¿Has visto a alguien?
No he visto a nadie

Adverbs of location

aquí	here	**cerca**	near
allí	there	**fuera**	outside
dentro/adentro	inside	**detrás**	behind
arriba	upstairs	**debajo**	under
delante	in front of	**encima**	(on) top
lejos	far	**allá**	over there

Adverbs of time

ahora	now	**entonces**	then
ayer	yesterday	**hoy**	today
luego	later	**después**	later on
nunca	never	**siempre**	always
temprano	early	**tarde**	late

Ya; aún no/todavía no

In order to express that something has already been done, the word **ya** is used

¿Has leído ya el libro?
Todavía no/aún no

Ya he visitado todos los monumentos

Cardinal numbers

0 cero	11 once	21 veintiuno	40 cuarenta
1 uno/a	12 doce	22 veintidós	41 cuarenta y uno
2 dos	13 trece	23 veintitrés	50 cincuenta
3 tres	14 catorce	24 veinticuatro	60 sesenta
4 cuatro	15 quince	25 veinticinco	70 setenta
5 cinco	16 dieciséis	26 veintiséis	80 ochenta
6 seis	17 diecisiete	27 veintisiete	90 noventa
7 siete	18 dieciocho	28 veintiocho	100 cien
8 ocho	19 diecinueve	29 veintinueve	101 ciento uno
9 nueve	20 veinte	30 treinta	140 ciento cuarenta
10 diez			

200 doscientos/as	800 ochocientos/as
215 doscientos/as quince	900 novecientos/as
300 trescientos/as	1000 mil
400 cuatrocientos/as	1250 mil doscientos/as cincuenta
500 quinientos/as	100.000 cien mil
600 seiscientos/as	1.000.000 un millón
700 setecientos/as	2.000.000 dos millones

Un is used with **millón** but not with **mil**

Ordinal numbers

primer/o	sexto
segundo	séptimo
tercer/o	octavo
cuarto	noveno
quinto	décimo

Note that **primero** and **tercero** lose the **o** before a masculine noun.

Key to exercises

Lesson 1

Exercise 1

1 Soy Brian, el hermano de Max 2 Soy Stella, la hermana de Laura
3 Soy Carmen, la hermana de Teresa 4 Soy Teresa, la hermana de
Juan 5 Soy Juan, el hermano de Teresa 6 Soy Claudio, el hermano
de Juan

Exercise 3

1 ¿Estás cansado/ocupado/enfermo/libre? 2 ¿Está tu hermano
cansado/ocupado/libre/enfermo? 3 ¿Está tu hermana cansada/
ocupada/enferma/libre?

Exercise 4

1 Estoy ocupado/a pero mi hermana está libre 2 Estoy cansado/a
pero mi hermano no está ocupado 3 Estoy libre pero mi hermana
está enferma 4 Mi hermano no está libre y yo estoy enfermo/a
5 Estoy ocupado/a y mi hermana está cansada

Exercise 6

1 ¿Qué tal el viaje? 2 ¿Qué tal la película? 3 ¿Qué tal la fiesta?
4 ¿Qué tal tu hermana?

Exercise 8

1 ésta es la madre de Arantxa 2 éste es el hermano de Carmen
3 ésta es la hermana de José 4 éste es el padre de Carmen 5 ésta
es Carmen, la amiga española de Sonia

Exercise 11

1–f, 2–c, 3–d, 4–g, 5–b, 6–a, 7–h, 8–e

Exercise 12

1 no, es norteamericana. 2 no, es australiano. 3 no, es inglés. 4 no, es inglesa. 5 no, es neozelandesa. 6 no, es inglés

Exercise 13

francesa/americana/argentino/brasileña/mejicano/canadiense/irlandesa/escocés

Exercise 14

ocupado/vale/oficina/jefe/casa/película

Exercise 15

1–d, 2–g, 3–a, 4–e, 5–f, 6–c, 7–b, 8–h

Reading

1 She is with a friend 2 The journey was good 3 They are going to María's house

Lesson 2

Exercise 2

1 Toledo está en el centro 2 Valencia está en el este 3 Jaén está en el sur 4 Santander está en el norte 5 Vitoria está en el norte 6 Tarragona está en el este

Exercise 11

1–c, 2–f, 3–e, 4–a, 5–b, 6–d

Reading

1–V, 2–F, 3–V, 4–F, 5–V

Lesson 3

Exercise 1

1 al   2 a la   3 a la   4 a la   5 al   6 al

Exercise 3

1 Voy   2 Va   3 Vas   4 Voy   5 Va

Exercise 4

1 este   2 éste   3 esta   4 esta   5 ésta

Exercise 5

1–c, 2–e, 3–f, 4–a, 5–b, 6–d

Exercise 7

1 ¿Cómo está usted? Muy bien, y ¿usted?   2 ¿De dónde es usted?
De Edimburgo, y ¿usted?   3 ¿Cuántas lenguas habla usted? Dos,
inglés y español, y ¿usted?   4 Betty, ¿tiene usted hermanos? Una
hermana, y ¿usted?

Exercise 8

1 ¿De dónde eres?   2 ¿Adónde vas/va?   3 ¿Cuántas lenguas
hablas/a?   4 ¿Cómo estás/á?   5 ¿Tiene fax?   6 ¿Es ésa tu/su
maleta?

Exercise 9

1 ¿Tiene una habitación doble, por favor?   2 ¿Tiene una habitación
doble?   3 ¿Tiene dos habitaciones dobles, una con cama de matri-
monio y otra con dos camas?   4 ¿Tiene una habitación triple?
5 ¿Tiene una habitación individual?   6 ¿Tiene cinco habitaciones
individuales?

Exercise 12

1 como   2 vives   3 está, trabaja   4 soy, vivo   5 habla   6 viajas

Exercise 13

¿Cúanto cuesta ese plato/esa taza/ese cenicero/ese cuadro/esa muñeca?

Exercise 14

1–d, 2–f, 3–a, 4–h, 5–g, 6–c, 7–b, 8–e

Exercise 15

1–e, 2–d, 3–a, 4–b, 5–c, 6–g, 7–f

Reading

1 He wants the room for four nights 2 He wants two rooms, one single and one double

Lesson 4

Exercise 1

1–c

Exercise 3

At the door, turn right, take the third street on the left, San Miguel street, cross the square, and the library is in the same street, on the right.

Exercise 4

¿Dónde está la estación de ferrocarril/la oficina de turismo/una librería/un supermercado/un banco/la embajada australiana?

Exercise 6

1–b, 2–e, 3–c, 4–a, 5–f, 6–d

Exercise 7

1 sabes 2 puedes 3 conozco 4 sé 5 sabe 6 conoces 7 puede
8 sé 9 sabe 10 conoce

Exercise 8

1 sí   2 la línea quinta   3 la línea cuarta   4 no

Exercise 11

1 ¿Puedo ir al cine?   2 ¿Puedo escribir a mi hermano?

Exercise 12

1–e, 2–d, 3–f, 4–b, 5–c, 6–g, 7–a

Exercise 13

Un dólar vale quinientos ochenta y siète pesos chilenos
Un dólar vale seiscientos noventa y nueve bolivares venezolanos
Un dólar vale dos reales brasileños

Lesson 5

Exercise 2

1 sale a las tres y media   2 sale a las seis menos cuarto   3 no hay trenes para Barcelona   4 no, sale después de las cuatro   5 llega a las nueve de la noche   6 llega a las seis y media

Exercise 5

1–c, 2–e, 3–f, 4–a, 5–d, 6–b

Exercise 7

1 Pedro se va de vacaciones   2 Luisa no se va a Inglaterra   3 Me voy a Nueva York mañana

Exercise 8

tienes/tengo/tengo/tienes/tengo

Exercise 11

1–f, 2–e, 3–a, 4–b, 5–c, 6–d

Exercise 12

1–f, 2–e, 3–b, 4–a, 5–d, 6–c, 7–g

Reading

1 Up to 329 passengers can travel 2 Prices depend on the class and on the time the journey starts 3 It takes 2 hours 50 minutes

Lesson 6

Exercise 1

1–c, 2–a, 3–d, 4–e, 5–b

Exercise 2

1 acaba de venir 2 acabo de llamarle 3 acaba de irse 4 acabo de terminarlo 5 acabo de leerlo 6 acaba de salir

Exercise 6

1 qué 2 qué 3 cuál 4 cuál 5 qué 6 qué 7 cúal 8 cuál

Exercise 11

verduras	*pescado*	*carne*	*fruta*
espárragos	merluza	chuletas de cerdo	naranjas
tomates	anchoas	filete de vaca	plátano
coliflor	sardinas	pollo	uvas
judías verdes	atún		manzanas

Reading

1 It is in Madrid 2 The sandwich of shoulder of pork with cheese 3 They cost dos euros 4 It closes at 6 a.m.

Lesson 7

Exercise 2

1–e, 2–d, 3–b, 4–f, 5–a, 6–c

Exercise 4

1–c, 2–e, 3–f, 4–a, 5–d, 6–b

Exercise 5

Susan, I am at the 'San Lorenzo' hospital because Pedrito has a really bad headache. If you arrive early, please prepare something for dinner; I think there are some lamb chops in the freezer. If I am not home before eight o'clock, call my husband at the office, and tell him where I am. Thanks.

Exercise 7

trae/vuelva/llama/llame/ponga/escribe/escriba

Exercise 9

1–d, 2–c, 3–e, 4–a, 5–b

Exercise 10

1 ¿Vengo luego? 2 ¿Lo hago ahora? 3 ¿Lo traigo ahora? 4 ¿Vuelvo luego? 5 ¿La escribo mañana? 6 ¿Le llamo ahora?

Exercise 12

1–b, 2–d, 3–e, 4–a, 5–c, 6–f

Exercise 13

1 brazo, muñeca, codo, cuello, espalda, costillas, dedos 2 rodilla, tobillo, cadera, fémur, dedos, pierna

Reading

1 He has no pain 2 He doesn't do any kind of exercise. He goes once in a while to the mountains 3 The doctor advised him to stop smoking and drinking, to do some form of exercise and, if possible, to go to live in the country

Horoscope

1 Aries, Gemini, Virgo, Sagittarius, and Pisces will all have good health 2 Taurus will have stomach problems 3 Capricorn will have headaches

Lesson 8

Exercise 1

1–c, 2–e, 3–f, 4–a, 5–d, 6–b

Exercise 6

The pop star and actress, Madonna

Exercise 11

1 muchos   2 muy   3 muchas   4 mucho   5 muchos   6 mucho
7 muy   8 muy

Exercise 12

la cocina	*el comedor*	*el dormitorio*	*el salón*	*el estudio*
armario	mesa	armario	sofá	mesa
mesa	sillas	mesilla de noche	butacas	sillas
sillas	lámpara	lámpara	lámpara	lámpara
cocina de gas	cuadros	cama	cuadros	librería
lavadora	espejo	cuadros	espejo	ordenador
lavavajillas		espejo		cuadros
nevera		cómoda		impresora
horno				

Exercise 13

limpiabotas/tocadiscos/paraguas/parabrisas/sacacorchos.

Reading

1 It is only a hundred metres from the beach   2 The kitchen, the dining room, and the sitting room   3 Lesley's friends own it

Lesson 9

Exercise 1

1–c, 2–d, 3–b, 4–a, 5–f, 6–e

Exercise 2

1 Ya la echo yo 2 Ya voy yo 3 Ya la pongo yo 4 Ya las termino yo 5 Ya la abro yo 6 Ya la grabo yo 7 Ya voy yo 8 Ya friego yo

Exercise 8

1 ¿Dígame/diga? 2 ¿De parte de quién? 3 Ahora le pongo

Exercise 10

1–d, 2–g, 3–c, 4–e, 5–f, 6–b, 7–a

Exercise 11

1–e, 2–d, 3–f, 4–a, 5–b, 6–c

Reading

1 There is a problem with his car 2 Because he is studying for his exams 3 She could be a lecturer or a teacher

Lesson 10

Exercise 1

1–f, 2–c, 3–e, 4–b, 5–a, 6–d

Exercise 5

1–d, 2–c, 3–b, 4–e, 5–a

Exercise 6

1 Sí, ya la he hecho 2 Sí, ya la he preparado 3 Sí, ya las he comprado 4 Sí, ya la he planchado 5 Sí, ya los he preparado 6 Sí, ya les he llamado

Exercise 7

1–h, 2–d, 3–e, 4–f, 5–b, 6–g, 7–a, 8–c

Exercise 8

1 Tengo sueño 2 Tengo hambre 3 Tengo frío 4 Tengo calor
5 Tengo sed 6 Tengo prisa

Exercise 11

Thanks a lot for the invitation, but I am not going to be able to come because my mum is ill and will have to spend a few weeks in hospital. As usual I have to look after my brothers. I am sorry. If you don't mind I could come at Easter. What do you think? Write soon.

Exercise 12

1–c, 2–f, 3–a, 4–e, 5–b, 6–d

Exercise 13

1–c, 2–f, 3–h, 4–j, 5–a, 6–i, 7–d, 8–b, 9–f, 10–e

Reading

1 Because she met a friend outside the cinema 2 She has broken up with her boyfriend 3 He is in Sevilla

Lesson 11

Exercise 1

1–c, 2–e, 3–d, 4–f, 5–b, 6–a

Exercise 2

1 Los compré _____
2 Lo vi _____
3 Se lo di _____
4 Se lo mandé _____
5 Me la compró _____
6 La construyeron _____

Exercise 5

No puedes imaginarte qué desastre de viaje. Perdí el último tren así que tuve que ir a dedo. Una mujer muy simpática paró pero en medio del camino el coche se averió. Conseguimos un mecánico aunque eran las doce de la noche. Tardó en arreglarlo más de dos horas. Por fin volvimos a la carretera. Llegamos a Barcelona a las nueve y media. Perfecto: la conferencia empezaba a las diez, pero no. ¡Después de todo, la conferencia se había cancelado porque el conferenciante estaba enfermo!

Exercise 7

Hola Sonia:
¿Cómo te va todo? Estoy ahora en un pueblo cerca de Bilbao. La semana pasada estuve con los amigos de Luisa. Fui con ellos a Lequeitio, ¿lo conoces? Es un pueblo muy bonito. Cominos muchísimas gambas. Ya sabes cuánto me gustan. Después me llevaron a las fiestas de Bermeo, ¡Qué fiestas! Estuvimos allí hasta las seis de la mañana. Hasta pronto,

Exercise 8

1 Quedamos en que te llamaría _____ 2 Quedamos en que le escribiría _____ 3 Quedamos en que se lo diría _____ 4 Quedamos en que hablaría con el _____ 5 Quedamos en que iría _____ 6 Quedamos en que lo haría _____

Exercise 10

1–e, 2–c, 3–d, 4–b, 5–a

Exercise 12

1–e, 2–f, 3–h, 4–g, 5–b, 6–c, 7–a, 8–d

Exercise 13

1 Por lo tanto 2 Por si 3 Por casualidad 4 Por lo demás 5 Por eso 6 Por suerte 7 Por cierto 8 Por fin 9 Por poco

Reading

1 He was a waiter, a soldier, and a writer   2 He was captured by the Turks   3 It was an unhappy marriage

Lesson 12

Exercise 5

1–e, 2–c, 3–a, 4–b, 5–f, 6–d

Exercise 10

1 Soy Antonio   2 Muy bien, y ¿tú? 3 ¿Dónde estuviste anoche? 4 ¿Estuviste sola?   5 ¿Qué hicisteis?   6 ¿A qué hora se fue?   7 ¿Te apetece ir a tomar una copa?   8 ¿A las diez?

Exercise 12

1–d, 2–g, 3–f, 4–h, 5–a, 6–e, 7–c, 8–b

Exercise 13

past	*present*	*future*
anteayer	ahora mismo	mañana a mediodía
anoche	ahora	esta noche
anteanoche		esta tarde
hace unas horas		mañana por la mañana

Reading

It has been booked for a week from the 15th of August. It does not have a sea view.

Lesson 13

Exercise 1

Jugar	*Ver*	*Salir*	*Vivir*	*Pasor*	*Leer*
Jugaba	veía	salía	vivía	pasaba	leía
jugabas	veías	salías	vivías	pasabas	leías
jugaba	veía	salía	vivía	pasaba	leía

Exercise 5

1 quien 2 que 3 quien 4 que 5 quien

Exercise 6

1–c, 2–e, 3–a, 4–b, 5–f, 6–d

Exercise 8

Estaba/oí/salí/salía/vi/Era/tenía/Llevaba/tenía/estaba/Fui

Exercise 9

alto/a-bajo/a,   tranquilo/a-nervioso/a,   simpático/a-antipático/a,
guapo/a-feo/a,   agradable-desagradable

Exercise 11

desear-deseable/temer-temible/perder-perdedor/servir-servible,
útil/razonar-razonable/vencer-vencedor/soñar-soñador/lavar-
lavable

Lesson 14

Exercise 1

1–b, 2–d, 3–f, 4–c, 5–a, 6–e

Exercise 6

1–b, 2–e, 3–d, 4–a, 5–c

Exercise 7

1 No, pero iré luego 2 No, pero lo leeré otro día 3 No, pero le
escribiré pronto 4 No, pero lo sabré luego 5 No, pero los tendré
esta tarde 6 No, pero hablaré con él más tarde

Exercise 8

1 no están listos   2 no está lista   3 no está listo   4 no está listo   5 no están listas

Exercise 9

Thanks for the invitation. I will arrive at Gatwick airport on the 16th of July at 4 p.m. I will come with a friend who speaks English so don't worry about coming to Gatwick. I will take a taxi from Victoria station. Will you be at home that afternoon? If there is any problem, call me.

Exercise 10

imposible, incómodo, inadecuado, incurable, incapaz, inexperto, incierto, infeliz, incoherente, injusto, ilegítimo, ilimitado, ilógico.

Reading

1 He needs Carmina's daughter's love   2 His father will first be a draughtsman, whilst the son will be a quantity surveyor   3 He will write a poetry book

Lesson 15

Exercise 1

trabajas/duermo/probable/raro

Exercise 2

No creo que esté estudiando/No creo que esté en casa/No creo que vaya mañana/No creo que viva en esa casa/No creo que trabaje en la embajada/No creo que salga con Dolores

Exercise 3

Quiero que llames a la oficina/Quiero que llames al médico/Quiero que compres algo de fruta/Quiero que prepares una tortilla

Exercise 5

1 Espero que apruebes los exámenes de español   2 Espero que veas a Lourdes   3 Espero que aprendas a conducir   4 Espero que compres un coche pronto   5 Espero que encuentres una casa pronto   6 Espero que vengas de nuevo

Exercise 9

Welcome to Llanes. I hope you have a good time and that the weather is good so that you can go on the beach. I know how much you like it! When you arrive, go to the neighbour's house (the one with the balcony full of flowers), and tell them that you have arrived. They know you are coming. Please, when you leave the house at night close all the windows well (there have been a lot of burglaries in the area lately).
I'll see you on the 15th of August.

Exercise 11

acostado/levantado/dormido/sentado/vestido/peinado/preocupado

Spanish–English glossary

Unless nouns have the letters *m* (masculine) or *f* (feminine) next to them, those that end in **o** are masculine and those that end in **a** are feminine.

a	to, at, on	**acostarse**	to go to bed
a las ...	at ... o'clock	**actor**(*m*)	actor
abajo	below	**actriz**(*f*)	actress
abanico	fan	**actual**	present-day
abierto(a)	open	**actuar**	to act
abogado	lawyer	**acuerdo**	agreement
abrazo	hug	**acusar**	to accuse
abrelatas(*m*)	tin opener	**adecuado(a)**	appropriate
abrigo	coat	**adelantar**	to advance, to
abril	April		overtake
abrir	to open	**adelgazar**	to lose weight
absuelto(a)	absolved	**además**	besides
abuelo/a	grandfather/	**adentro**	inside
	mother	**adiós**	goodbye
aburrido(a)	bored/boring	**adjunto(a)**	attached
acabar	to finish	**¿adónde?**	where (to)?
acabar de	to have just	**adornar**	to decorate, to
	(done		adorn
	something)	**aduana**	customs
acacia	acacia	**adulto(a)**	adult
accidente(*m*)	accident	**aéreo(a)**	air
aceite(*m*)	oil	**aeropuerto**	airport
aceituna	olive	**afeitarse**	to shave
acera	pavement	**afuera**	outside
acerca	about	**agarrar**	to seize
acompañar	to go with	**agencia**	estate agency
acordarse	to remember	**inmobilaria**	

agitar	to shake	**América**	America
agosto	August	**amigo(a)**	friend
agotar	to exhaust	**amor**(*m*)	love
agradable	pleasant	**ancho(a)**	wide
agradecer	to thank	**anchoa**	anchovy
agua(*m*)	water	**andaluz**(*m*)	Andalusian
agua corriente	running water	**andar**	to walk
agua potable	drinking water	**andén**(*m*)	platform
aguacate(*m*)	avocado	**anillo**	ring
aguja	needle	**anoche**	last night
ahí	there	**anochecer**	to get dark
ahogar	to drown	**anochecer**(*m*)	nightfall
ahora	now	**anteanoche**	the night before last
ahorrar	to save		
aire(*m*)	air	**anteayer**	the day before last
ajo	garlic		
al	at the	**antes de**	before
al borde	at the edge	**antipático(a)**	unfriendly
alcalde(*m*)	mayor	**anuncio**	advertisement
alegrarse	to be happy	**añadir**	to add
alegre	happy	**año**	year
alemán/alemana	German	**apagar**	to switch off
Alemania	Germany	**aparato**	set
alfombra	rug	**aparcar**	to park
algo	something	**aparejador**	quantity surveyor
algodón(*m*)	cotton		
alguien	someone	**apartamento**	flat
alguno(a)	some	**apellido**	surname
alimentar	to feed	**apetecer**	to feel like
almorzar	to have lunch	**apostar**	to bet
alojamiento	accommodation	**apresar**	to seize
alojarse	to stay, to lodge	**aprobar**	to pass an exam
allí	there	**aproximadamente**	approximately
alquilar	to rent	**a punto**	ready
alquiler(*m*)	rent	**aquí**	here
alto(a)	tall	**árbol**(*m*)	tree
ama de casa	housewife	**armario**	cupboard
amable	kind	**arreglar**	to repair
amar	to love	**arriba**	above
amargo(a)	bitter	**arroz**(*m*)	rice
ambicioso(a)	ambitious	**artículo**	article
ambiente(*m*)	atmosphere	**asado(a)**	roast

asar	to roast	**biblioteca**	library
ascensor(*m*)	lift	**bicicleta**	bicycle
así	like this	**bien**	well
así que	so that	**bienvenido(a)**	welcome
aspirina	aspirin	**billete**(*m*)	ticket
asunto	issue, affair	**blanco**	white
ataque(*m*)	attack, fit	**boca**	mouth
atentamente	faithfully (in a letter)	**bocadillo**	sandwich
		bocata(*m*)	sandwich
atrás	behind	**boda**	wedding
atravesar	to cross	**boli, bolígrafo**	pen
atún(*m*)	tuna	**bolso**	handbag
aún	yet	**bombilla**	light bulb
aunque	although	**bonito(a)**	pretty
autobús(*m*)	bus	**bota**	boot
autopista	motorway	**botella**	bottle
azúcar(*m*)	sugar	**brazo**	arm
a veces	sometimes	**brillar**	to shine
avería	breakdown (*car*)	**broma**	joke
averiado(a)	broken down	**brutalidad**(*f*)	brutality
avión(*m*)	aeroplane	**buenas noches**	good night
avisar	to warn	**buenas tardes**	good afternoon
ayer	yesterday	**bueno(a)**	good
ayudar	to help	**buenos días**	good morning
ayuntamiento	town hall	**buscar**	to look for
azul	blue	**buzón**(*m*)	letterbox
bacalao	cod	**caballo**	horse
bailar	to dance	**cabeza**	head
bajar	to go down	**cabina**	telephone box
bajo(a)	short	**cada**	each
balón(*m*)	ball	**cadera**	hip
bañarse	to bathe/to swim	**caerse**	to fall
bañera	bath	**café**(*m*)	coffee
baño	bath	**cafetería**	bar
bar(*m*)	bar	**caja**	box
barato(a)	cheap	**calcetines**(*mpl*)	socks
barco	boat	**caldo**	clear soup
barra	stick (bread)	**calefacción**(*f*)	heating
barrio	neighbourhood	**calentar**	to heat up
bastante	enough	**caliente**	hot, warm
bata	dressing gown	**callarse**	to shut up
beber	to drink	**calle**(*f*)	street

cama	bed	**cerillas**	matches
cámara	camera	**cerrado(a)**	closed
camarero	waiter	**cerrar**	to shut
cambiar	to change	**cerveza**	beer
camino	way	**cien**	hundred
camión(*m*)	lorry	**cierto**	true
camisa	shirt	**cigarro**	cigarette
camiseta	T-shirt	**cinco**	five
campana	bell	**cincuenta**	fifty
campaña	campaign	**cine**(*m*)	cinema
camping(*m*)	camp site	**cinturón**(*m*)	belt
campo	countryside	**cita**	appointment
cana	white hair	**ciudad**(*f*)	city
canadiense	Canadian	**claro**	clear, of course
cancelar	to cancel	**cliente**(*m, f*)	client
cansado(a)	tired	**clima**(*m*)	climate
caña	glass (beer)	**cobrar**	to earn
capaz	able	**cocina**	kitchen
cara	face	**cocinar**	to cook
cariño	affection/darling	**coche**(*m*)	car
carne(*f*)	meat	**coger**	to get, to catch
carnet de		**coherente**	coherent
conducir(*m*)	driving licence	**cola**	queue
caro(a)	expensive	**colegio**	school
carpintero	carpenter	**coliflor**(*f*)	cauliflower
carretera	road	**color**(*m*)	colour
carta	letter	**comedor**(*m*)	dining-room
cartera	wallet	**comenzar**	to start
casa	house	**cometer**	to commit
casado(a)	married	**comida**	meal
casarse	to get married	**comisaría**	police station
casi	nearly	**¿cómo?**	how?
catedral	cathedral	**como**	as, like
categoría	category/class	**cómodo(a)**	comfortable
catorce	fourteen	**compañero(a)**	companion/
cautivo	captive		friend
cebolla	onion	**compartir**	to share
cena	dinner	**comprar**	to buy
cenar	to have dinner	**comprobar**	to check
cenicero	ashtray	**comunicación**	communication
centro	centre	**comunicar**	to be engaged
cerca	near		(telephone)

con	with	**cuero**	leather
concierto	concert	**cuerpo**	body
conducir	to drive	**cueva**	cave
conferencia	conference	**¡cuidado!**	be careful!
congelador(*m*)	freezer	**cuidar**	to look after
conmigo	with me	**cumpleaños**(*m*)	birthday
conocer	to know	**curable**	curable
conseguir	to obtain	**chaqueta**	jacket
construir	to build	**charlar**	to chat
contento(a)	happy	**cheque de**	traveller's
contestar	to answer	**viaje**(*m*)	cheque
convertir	to turn, to	**chica**	girl
	change	**chico**	boy
convivencia	living together	**chino**	Chinese
copa	glass, a drink	**chocolate**(*m*)	chocolate
corbata	tie	**chuleta**	chop
cordero	lamb	**dar**	to give
correos(*m*)	post office	**darse cuenta**	to realize
corrida de toros	bullfight	**de**	of, from
corto(a)	short	**deberes**(*mpl*)	homework
cosa	thing	**débil**	weak
coser	to sew	**decir**	to say
costa	coast	**de crucero**	cruising (*speed*)
costar	to cost	**dedo**	finger
costilla	rib	**dejar**	to leave
creer	to believe, think	**dejar de**	to stop (doing
crema	cream		something)
cruzar	to cross	**delante de**	in front of
cuaderno	notebook	**deletrear**	to spell
cuadro	picture	**delineante**	draughtsman
¿cuál?	which? what?	**demasiado**	too much
¿cuándo?	when?	**dentista**(*m, f*)	dentist
cuando	when	**dentro**	inside
¿cuánto?	how much?	**depende**	depends
cuarenta	forty	**deportes**(*mpl*)	sports
cuarto	a quarter	**deportista**(*m, f*)	sports person
cuarto de baño	bathroom	**derecha**	right
cuatro	four	**desagradable**	unpleasant
cubano(a)	Cuban	**desastre**	disaster
cuchara	spoon	**desayunar**	to have
cuchillo	knife		breakfast
cuenta	bill	**desayuno**	breakfast

descansar	to rest	**documento**	document
descuento	discount	**doler**	to ache
desde	from	**dolor**	pain
desde luego	of course	**domicilio**	residence
desear	to wish	**domingo**	Sunday
despacio	slowly	**don**	Mr
despedirse	to say goodbye	**doña**	Mrs
despejado(a)	clear	**¿dónde?**	where?
despertarse	to wake up	**dormir**	to sleep
después	afterwards	**dormitorio**	bedroom
detrás	behind	**doscientos**	two hundred
de verdad	truly	**ducha**	shower
día(m)	day	**dueño**	owner
dibujar	to draw	**dulce**	sweet
diciembre	December	**durante**	during
diecinueve	nineteen	**durar**	to last
dieciocho	eighteen	**duro**	five pesetas
dieciséis	sixteen	**duro(a)**	hard
diecisiete	seventeen	**echar**	to pour/to throw
diez	ten	**echar en falta**	to miss (*people*)
difícil	difficult	**edad**(f)	age
dinero	money	**edificio**	building
dirección(f)	address/ direction	**ejecutivo(a)**	executive
director(m)	director/ manager	**ejemplo**	example
		ejercicio	exercise
disco	record	**el**	the
discoteca	discothèque	**él**	he
disculpa	apology	**elegante**	smart
discutir	to argue	**ella**	she
discusión(f)	discussion, argument	**ellas**	they(f)
		ellos	they(m)
disfrutar	to enjoy	**empezar**	to start
disponible	available	**emprender**	to undertake
distinto(a)	different	**empresa**	firm
divertido(a)	funny	**en**	in, on
divertirse	to enjoy	**enamorado(a)**	in love
divorciado(a)	divorced	**en cambio**	on the other hand
divorciarse	to divorce		
doble(m)	double	**encantado(a)**	delighted
doce	twelve	**encarcelar**	to imprison
documental(m)	documentary	**encima de**	on top of
		encontrar	to find

encontrarse	to bump into somebody	**éste(a)**	this one
enero	January	**estéril**	sterile
enfadarse	to get annoyed	**esto**	this
enfermera	nurse	**estos**	these
enfermo(a)	ill	**éstos**	these ones
enfrente	opposite	**estrecho(a)**	narrow
en general	generally	**estrella**	star
¡enhorabuena!	congratulations!	**estricto(a)**	strict
ensalada	salad	**estudiante**(*m, f*)	student
enseñar	to show/ to teach	**estudiar**	to study
		estupendo(a)	marvellous
entonces	then	**euro**	euro
entrada	ticket (cinema)/ entrance	**examen**(*m*)	exam
		excesos(*mpl*)	excess
entrar	to enter	**excursión**(*f*)	excursion
entrevista	interview	**éxito**	success
enviar	to send	**experto(a)**	expert
equipaje(*m*)	luggage	**extranjero**	foreigner
equivocarse	to be mistaken	**fábrica**	factory
escalera	staircase	**fácil**	easy
escándalo	scandal	**falda**	skirt
escenario	stage	**falta**	mistake
escocés/escocesa	Scottish	**fallecer**	to die
escribir	to write	**familia**	family
ese	that	**farmacia**	chemist
eso	that	**febrero**	February
esos	those	**fecha**	date
espalda	back (body)	**felicitar**	to congratulate
español(a)	Spanish	**feliz**	happy
espárragos(*mpl*)	asparagus	**ferretería**	ironmonger's shop
especialista(*m, f*)	specialist		
esperar	to wait	**fiel**	faithful
espiar	to spy	**fiesta**	fiesta, party
espontáneo(a)	spontaneous	**fijo(a)**	fixed
esquina	corner	**filete**(*m*)	fillet
estable	stable	**filtro**	filter
estación(*f*)	station	**final**(*m*)	end
estanco	tobacconist	**fin de semana**(*m*)	weekend
estar	to be	**firma**	signature
este	east	**físico(a)**	physical
este(a)	this	**flor**(*f*)	flower
		fraile(*m*)	monk

francés/francesa	French	**guerra**	war
frase(*f*)	sentence	**guía**(*m, f*)	guide
frecuente	frequent	**guía telefónica**	telephone
fregar	to wash up		directory
freír	to fry	**gustar**	to like
frío(a)	cold	**gusto**	taste
frito(a)	fried	**habitación**(*f*)	room, bedroom
frontera	frontier	**hablar**	to speak
fruta	fruit	**hacer**	to do
fuerte	strong	**hacer daño**	to hurt
fumar	to smoke	**hacer falta**	to need
funcionar	to work	**hacer sol**	to be sunny
	(*machines*)	**hacia**	towards
funcionario	civil servant	**hasta**	until, as far as
fútbol(*m*)	football	**hasta la vista**	until next time
gabardina	raincoat	**hasta luego**	see you later
gafas	glasses (*eye*)	**hasta mañana**	see you
gallego(a)	Galician		tomorrow
galletas	biscuits	**hasta pronto**	see you soon
gama	range	**hay**	there is, there
gambas	prawns		are
ganar	to earn	**hecho**	done
garaje(*m*)	garage	**helada**	frost
gastar	to spend	**helado**	ice-cream
gato	cat	**hermano/a**	brother/sister
gente(*f*)	people	**hielo**	ice
geranio	geranium	**hija**	daughter
girar	to go round	**hijo**	son
girasol(*m*)	sunflower	**historia**	history
gitano	gipsy	**¡hola!**	hello!
golpe(*m*)	knock	**hombre**	man
gordo(a)	fat	**hora**	hour
gorra	peaked cap	**horario**	timetable
gracias	thanks	**hospital**(*m*)	hospital
gramo	gram	**hostal**(*m*)	hostel
grande	big	**hotel**(*m*)	hotel
grave	serious	**hoy**	today
gripe(*f*)	flu	**hueso**	bone
gris	grey	**huevo**	egg
gritar	to shout	**ida**	outward
guapo(a)	handsome/		journey
	beautiful	**idioma**(*m*)	language

igual	the same	**jersey**(*m*)	jersey
ilegítimo(a)	illegitimate	**joven**	young
ilimitado(a)	unlimited	**judías verdes**	green beans
ilógico(a)	illogical	**jueves**	Thursday
importar	to matter	**jugador**(*m*)	player
importante	important	**jugar**	to play
imposible	impossible	**juguete**(*m*)	toy
imprescindible	essential	**julio**	July
impresora	printer	**junio**	June
inadecuado(a)	unsuitable	**juntos**	together
incapaz	incapable	**justo(a)**	just/fair
incierto(a)	uncertain	**kilo**	kilo
incluso	even	**kilómetro**	kilometre
incoherente	incoherent	**la**	the
incómodo(a)	uncomfortable	**lacón**(*m*)	shoulder of pork
incomprensión(*f*)	incomprehension	**lado**	side
incurable	incurable	**ladrón**(*m*)	thief
inexperto(a)	inexperienced	**lago**	lake
infeliz	unhappy	**lamentar**	to regret
información(*f*)	information	**lámpara**	lamp
Inglaterra	England	**lápiz**(*m*)	pencil
inglés/inglesa	English	**largo(a)**	long
injusto(a)	unjust	**las**(*fpl*)	the
insoportable	unbearable	**lavabo**	washbasin
instalarse	to settle in	**lavadora**	washing machine
intentar	to try		
interesante	interesting	**lavar**	to wash
internacional	international	**lavarse**	to wash oneself
intérprete(*m, f*)	interpreter	**lección**(*f*)	lesson
invierno	winter	**leche**(*f*)	milk
invitar	to invite	**lechuga**	lettuce
ir	to go	**leer**	to read
isla	island	**legítimo(a)**	legitimate
izquierda	left	**lejano(a)**	far away
jabón(*m*)	soap	**lejos**	far
jamás	never	**lengua**	tongue/language
jamón(*m*)	ham	**les**	(to)you/ (to) them
japonés/japonesa	Japanese		
jarabe(*m*)	syrup	**letra**	letter (*alphabet*)
jardín(*m*)	garden	**levantarse**	to get up
jarrón(*m*)	vase	**ley**(*f*)	law
jefe(*m, f*)	boss	**libra**	pound

libre	free	**mandar**	to order
librería	bookshop	**mano**(*f*)	hand
libro	book	**manta**	blanket
limón(*m*)	lemon	**mantener**	to keep
limpiar	to clean	**mantequilla**	butter
lío	mess/problem	**manzana**	apple
liquidación(*f*)	sales	**mañana**	tomorrow/
lista	list		morning
listo(a)	clever/ready	**mar**(*m*)	sea
literatura	literature	**marcharse**	to leave
lo	the, that which,	**marido**	husband
	it, him	**marisco**	shellfish
loco(a)	crazy	**marrón**	brown
lógico(a)	logical	**martes**	Tuesday
Londres	London	**marzo**	March
los(*mpl*)	the	**más**	more
luchar	to fight	**matricularse**	to enrol
luego	later	**matrimonio**	married couple
lugar	place	**mayo**	May
lujo	luxury	**mayor**	elder, older
luna	moon	**mayoría**	most
lunes	Monday	**me**	me (reflexive
luto	mourning		pronoun)
luz(*f*)	light	**mecánico**	mechanic
llamar	to call, phone	**mechero**	lighter
llamarse	to be called	**médico**	doctor
llegada	arrival	**médico de**	general practi-
llegar	to arrive	**cabecera**	tioner, GP
llenar	to fill	**medio**	middle
lleno(a)	full	**mediodía**(*m*)	midday
llevar	to carry, wear,	**mejor**	better
	take	**mejorar**	to improve
llorar	to cry	**melocotón**(*m*)	peach
llover	to rain	**melón**(*m*)	melon
llovizna	drizzle	**menos**	less
lluvia	rain	**menú**(*m*)	menu
madera	wood	**merecer**	to deserve
madre(*f*)	mother	**merienda**	snack
madrugar	to get up early	**merluza**	hake
mal	unwell, ill	**mes**(*m*)	month
maleta	suitcase	**mesa**	table
malo(a)	bad	**mesilla de noche**	beside table

mesón(*m*)	a type of restaurant	**negocio**	business
metro	underground	**negro(a)**	black
mi	my	**nervios**	nerves
mí	me	**nervioso(a)**	nervous
miércoles	Wednesday	**nevar**	to snow
mil	thousand	**nevera**	fridge
millón(*m*)	million	**niebla**	fog
minuto	minute	**nieto/a**	grandson/ daughter
mío(a)	mine	**nieve**(*f*)	snow
mirar	to look	**niño**	child
mismo(a)	same	**no**	not/no
mochila	rucksack	**noche**(*f*)	night
moda	fashion	**nombre**(*m*)	name
molestar	to disturb	**nordeste**	northeast
moneda	coin	**norte**(*m*)	north
monitor(*m*)	monitor	**nos**	(to) us
montaña	mountain	**nosotros(as)**	we
montar en bici	to ride a bike	**Noruega**	Norway
moreno(a)	dark-haired/ dark-skinned	**noticias**	news
		novecientos(as)	nine hundred
mover	to move	**noventa**	ninety
muebles(*mpl*)	furniture	**noviembre**	November
muela	tooth	**novia**	girlfriend
muerto(a)	dead	**novio**	boyfriend
mujer	woman	**nube**(*f*)	cloud
mundo	world	**nublado**	cloudy
muñeca	doll/wrist	**nueve**	nine
museo	museum	**nuevo(a)**	new
música	music	**número**	number
muy	very	**nunca**	never
nacionalidad(*f*)	nationality	**o**	or
nacer	to be born	**obra**	play (*work*)
nada	nothing	**obrero**	workman
nadar	to swim	**octubre**	October
nadie	nobody	**ochenta**	eighty
naranja	orange	**ocho**	eight
nata	cream	**oeste**(*m*)	west
navaja	pocket knife	**oficina**	office
Navidad	Christmas	**ofrecer**	to offer
necesario(a)	necessary	**oír**	to hear
necesitar	to need	**ojo**	eye

olvidarse	to forget
opinión(*f*)	opinion
ordenador(*m*)	computer
oro	gold
oscuro(a)	dark
otoño	autumn
otra vez	again
otro(a)	another
padre(*m*)	father
padres(*pl*)	parents
pagar	to pay
página	page
país(*m*)	country
pájaro	bird
palabra	word
pálido(a)	pale
pan(*m*)	bread
panadería	bakery
pantalones(*mpl*)	trousers
papel(*m*)	paper
paquete(*m*)	packet
para	for
parabrisas(*m*)	windscreen
parada	stop
parador(*m*)	state-run hotel
paraguas(*m*)	umbrella
pararse	to stop
parecer	to seem
periódicamente	periodically
paro	unemployment
partido	match
pasado(a)	last
pasaporte(*m*)	passport
pasar	to spend
pasarlo bien/mal	to have a good/ bad time
pasatiempo	hobby
paseo	walk
paso	step
pastel(*m*)	cake
pastelería	pâtisserie
patatas	potatoes

paz(*f*)	peace
pecas	freckles
pedir	to ask for
pedido	order
peinarse	to do one's hair
película	film
peligroso	dangerous
pelo	hair
peluquería	hairdresser's
pena	pity
pensar	to think
pensión(*f*)	boarding-house
peña	rock/group of friends
peor	worse
pequeño(a)	small
pera	pear
perder	to lose/to miss (*bus*)
perfecto(a)	perfect
perfume(*m*)	perfume
periódico	newspaper
permanecer	to remain
pero	but
perro	dog
persona	person
pescado	fish
pescadería	fishmonger's
pescar	to fish
pez(*m*)	fish (*alive*)
piano	piano
pie(*m*)	foot
piedra	stone
piel(*m*)	skin
pierna	leg
pila	battery
pimienta	ground pepper
pimiento	pepper
pinchar	to puncture
pintar	to paint
pintarse	to put on one's make-up

piña	pineapple	**preocuparse**	to worry
piscina	swimming pool	**presentar**	to introduce
piso	flat, floor		(*people*)
plano	plan	**presupuesto**	estimate
planta	floor (*storey*)	**primavera**	spring
planta baja	ground floor	**primero(a)**	first
plata	silver	**primo/a**	cousin
plátano	banana	**principios (a)**	at the beginning
plato	dish, plate	**prisa (tener)**	to be in a hurry
playa	beach	**probar**	to taste, to try
plaza	square	**profesor**(*m*)	teacher
pobre	poor	**profesora**(*f*)	teacher
pobreza	poverty	**programa**(*m*)	programme
poco(a)	little	**pronto**	soon
poder	to be able	**provincia**	province
poesía	poetry	**próximo(a)**	next
política	politics	**proyectar**	to project
polvo	dust	**prudente**	cautious
pollo	chicken	**publicar**	to publish
poner	to put	**pueblo**	village
ponerse a	to start	**puente**(*m*)	bridge
por	by, for	**puerta**	door
por casualidad	by chance	**puerto**	port
por cierto	by the way	**pues**	well
por ejemplo	for example	**pulsera**	bracelet
por eso	that's why	**que**	that, which
por favor	please	**¿qué?**	what? which?
por fin	at last	**¡que aproveche!**	*bon appétit!*
por lo demás	besides that	**quedar**	to be, to remain
por lo tanto	therefore	**quedarse**	to stay
por poco	nearly	**quejarse**	to complain
¿por qué?	why?	**querer**	to want
porque	because	**querido(a)**	dear
por si acaso	just in case	**queso**	cheese
por suerte	luckily	**quien**	who
por supuesto	of course	**¿quién?**	who?
posible	possible	**quince**	fifteen
postre	dessert	**quinientos(as)**	five hundred
precio	price	**quinto(a)**	fifth
preferir	to prefer	**quizás**	perhaps
preguntar	to ask	**ración**(*f*)	portion
preocupado(a)	worried	**radio**(*f*)	radio

ramas	branches (*tree*)	sábana	sheet
rápido(a)	fast	saber	to know
raquítico(a)	weak	sacar	to bring out
rato	while	sacacorchos(*m*)	bottle opener
razón(*f*)	reason	sal (*f*)	salt
recado	message	salado/a	salty
receta	prescription, recipe	salario	salary
		salida	exit
recibir	to receive	salir	to go out
recibo	bill (*gas*, etc.)	salón(*m*)	sitting-room
recoger	to collect	salud(*f*)	health
recomendar	to recommend	saludar	to greet, to say hello
recordar	to remember		
recto(a)	straight	sardinas	sardines
recuerdo	souvenir	sastre(*m*)	tailor
regalar	to give	se	one, oneself
regalo	present	seco	dry
región(*f*)	region	secretaria	secretary
reina	queen	seguido (todo)	straight on
reírse	to laugh	seguir	to follow
rellenar	to fill in	según	according to
repetir	to repeat	segundo	second
rescatar	to recapture	seguro	sure, certain
reservar	to book	seis	six
respiratorio(a)	respiratory	sello	stamp
respuesta	answer	semana	week
restaurante(*m*)	restaurant	sencilla	single (room)
retraso	delay	sentarse	to sit down
reunión(*f*)	meeting	sentir	to feel
revista	magazine	señor(*m*)	Mr
rey(*m*)	king	señora	Mrs
rico(a) (ser)	rich	señorita	Miss
rico(a) (estar)	tasty	separado(a)	separated
riñón(*m*)	kidney	septiembre	September
robar	to steal, to rob	ser	to be
rodilla	knee	serio(a)	serious
rojo(a)	red	servicios	toilets
ropa	clothes	sesenta	sixty
rubio(a)	blond, blonde	setecientos(as)	seven hundred
rueda	wheel	setenta	seventy
ruido	noise	sevillano(a)	Sevillian
sábado	Saturday	sexto(a)	sixth

si	if	**suficiente**	enough
sí	yes	**Suiza**	Switzerland
siempre	always	**sur**(*m*)	south
siete	seven	**suroeste**(*m*)	southwest
significar	to mean	**suspender**	to fail
sin	without	**tabaco**	tobacco
sin embargo	on the other hand	**tacones**(*mpl*)	heels
		tal vez	perhaps
sistema(*m*)	system	**talla**	size
sitio	place	**también**	also
situado(a)	situated	**tampoco**	neither, nor
sobre(*m*)	envelope	**tan**	so
sobre	on	**tanto**	as much, so much
sobre todo	above all		
sol	sun	**tapas**	bar snacks
solamente	only	**taquilla**	ticket office
soldado	soldier	**tardar en**	to take (*time*)
solicitado	to be in demand	**tarde**	late
		tarde(*f*)	afternoon
solicitar	to request	**tarifa**	tariff, rate
solicitud(*f*)	application form	**tarjeta**	card
sólo	only	**tasca**	bar
solo(a)	alone	**taxista**(*m, f*)	taxi driver
soltera	spinster, single woman	**taza**	cup
		te	you (*reflexive pronoun*)
soltero	bachelor, single man		
		té(*m*)	tea
sombra	shade	**teatro**	theatre
sombrero	hat	**techo**	ceiling
soñar	to dream	**teléfono**	telephone
sopa	soup	**televisión**(*f*)	television
sorpresa	surprise	**temperatura**	temperature
su, sus	his, hers, one's, your, their	**templado(a)**	lukewarm
		temprano(a)	early
suave	soft	**tenedor**(*m*)	fork
subir	to go up	**tener**	to have
sucio(a)	dirty	**tenis**(*m*)	tennis
Suecia	Sweden	**tercero(a)**	third
sueldo	wages	**terminar**	to finish
suerte(*f*)	luck	**ti**	(to) you
sueño (tener)	to be sleepy	**tiempo**	weather, time
suerte(*f*)	luck	**tienda**	shop

tienda de campaña	tent
timbre(*m*)	door bell
tinto	red wine
tió/a	uncle/aunt
tobillo	ankle
tocar	to play (*an instrument*)
todavía	yet, still
todo	all
tomar	to take, to have
tomate(*m*)	tomato
tormenta	storm
tortilla	omelette
total	total
trabajar	to work
trabajo	work
traer	to bring
traje(*m*)	suit
traje de baño(*m*)	swim suit
tranquilo(a)	calm, quiet
transporte(*m*)	transport
trato	treatment
trayecto	distance, stretch
trece	thirteen
treinta	thirty
tren(*m*)	train
tres	three
trescientos(as)	three hundred
triste	sad
triunfo	victory
tu	your
tú	you (singular, familiar)
turco(a)	Turk
turista(*m, f*)	tourist
tutear	to talk using the **tú** form
último(a)	last
un(a)	a, an, one
universidad(*f*)	university
urgente	urgent
usar	to use
usted	you (formal)
ustedes	you (plural, formal)
utilizar	to use
uvas	grapes
vacaciones(*fpl*)	holidays
vagón(*m*)	carriage
valer	to cost
vale	OK
valiente	brave
valle(*m*)	valley
vaso	glass
vecino	neighbour
vegetal(*m*)	vegetable
vehículo	vehicle
veinte	twenty
veinticinco	twenty-five
velocidad(*f*)	speed
vender	to sell
venir	to come
vencer	to defeat
ventana	window
ver	to see
verano	summer
verdad(*f*)	truth
verde	green
verdura	vegetable
vestido	dress
vestirse	to get dressed
vez(*f*)	time, occasion
vía	track (railway)
viajar	to travel
viaje(*m*)	journey
viajero	passenger
vida	life
viejo(a)	old
viernes	Friday

viento	wind	**vuelo**	flight
vino	wine	**vuelta**	return (ticket)
visitar	to visit	**water**(*m*)	lavatory
vista	view	**y**	and
vitalidad(*f*)	vitality	**ya**	now/already
vivir	to live	**yo**	I
volver	to come back	**yogur**(*m*)	yoghurt
vosotros(as)	you (plural)	**zumo**	juice

English–Spanish glossary

English	Spanish	English	Spanish
a, an	un, una	ankle	el tobillo
above	encima	to annoy	molestar
abroad	el extranjero	another	otro(a)
to accompany	acompañar	to answer	contestar
to ache	doler	apartment	el piso
actor	el actor	apple	la manzana
address	la dirección	arm	el brazo
advise	aconsejar	to arrest	detener
aeroplane	el avión	arrival	la llegada
after	después de	to arrive	llegar
afternoon	la tarde	artist	el/la artista
afterwards	después	as	como
again	otra vez	to ask	preguntar
age	la edad	to ask for	pedir
agreeable	agradable	at	en
airport	el aeropuerto	at last	por fin, al fin
air terminal	la terminal	at once	en seguida
alarm clock	el despertador	at what time?	¿a qué hora?
all	todos(as)	aunt	la tía
almost	casi	autumn	el otoño
alone	solo(a)	bachelor	el soltero
already	ya	bad	malo(a)
also	también	bag	la bolsa
although	aunque	ball	la pelota
always	siempre	bank	el banco
American	americano(a)	bar	el bar
amusing	divertido(a)	basketball	el baloncesto
and	y	Basque	vasco(a)
Andalusia	Andalucía	Basque Country	Euskadi
Andalusian	andaluz(a)	bathroom	el cuarto de
animal	el animal		baño

battery	**la pila**	brother	**el hermano**
to be	**ser/estar**	brown	**marrón**
to be able	**poder**	building	**el edificio**
to be careful	**tener cuidado**	bus	**el autobús**
to be hungry	**tener hambre**	bus stop	**la parada de**
to be thirsty	**tener sed**		**autobús**
beach	**la playa**	but	**pero**
beautiful (*woman*)	**guapa**	to buy	**comprar**
because	**porque**	café	**la cafetería**
bed	**la cama**	cake	**el pastel**
bedroom	**el dormitorio**	camera	**la cámara**
beer	**la cerveza**	campsite	**el camping**
before	**antes de**	capital	**la capital**
to begin to	**empezar a**	car	**el coche**
behind	**detrás/detrás de**	careful!	**¡cuidado!**
to believe	**creer**	to carry	**llevar**
beside	**al lado de**	cashier	**la/el cajera/o**
best	**el/la mejor**	Castilian	**castellano(a)**
better	**mejor**	cat	**el gato**
between	**entre**	Catalan	**catalán/catalana**
bicycle	**la bicicleta**	cathedral	**la catedral**
big	**grande**	central heating	**la calefacción**
bird	**el pájaro**		**central**
birthday	**el cumpleaños**	centre	**el centro**
black	**negro(a)**	century	**el siglo**
blanket	**la manta**	certain (*adv*)	**cierto**
blond, blonde	**rubio(a)**	chair	**la silla**
blue	**azul**	change	**el cambio**
boat	**el barco**	to change	**cambiar**
book	**el libro**	cheap	**barato(a)**
bookshop	**la librería**	cheese	**el queso**
boot	**la bota, el**	chemist's	**la farmacia**
	maletero (*car*)	child	**el niño/la niña**
boring	**aburrido(a)**	children	**los niños**
boss	**el/la jefe**	chocolate	**el chocolate**
bottle	**la botella**	to choose	**elegir**
brake	**el freno**	Christmas	**la Navidad**
to break	**romper**	church	**la iglesia**
breakfast	**el desayuno**	cigarette	**el cigarrillo**
briefcase	**la cartera**	cinema	**el cine**
to bring	**traer**	to clean	**limpiar**
broken	**roto(a)**	climate	**el clima**

clock	el reloj	to desire	desear
to close	cerrar	despite	a pesar de
closed	cerrado(a)	to dial	marcar
clothes	la ropa	different	distinto(a)
coast	la costa	to dine	cenar
coat	el abrigo	dining-room	el comedor
coffee	el café	dinner	la cena
coin	la moneda	director	el director/la
cold	frío(a)		directora
colour	el color	to disappear	desaparecer
to come	venir	to do	hacer
company	la compañía, la	doctor	el, la médico
	empresa	dog	el perro
to complain	quejarse	door	la puerta
computer	el ordenador	double	doble
to cook	cocinar	to dream	soñar
to cost	costar	dress	el vestido
country	el país	to dress	vestirse
countryside	el campo	to drink	beber, tomar
couple	la pareja	a toast	brindar
course	el curso	to drive	conducir
of course!	¡claro!	driving licence	el permiso de
cousin	el primo/la		conducir
	prima	dry	seco(a)
cream	la nata	during	durante
credit card	la tarjeta de	each	cada
	crédito	ear	la oreja
cup	la taza	earache	el dolor de
cupboard	el armario		oídos
currency	las divisas	early	temprano(a)
Customs	la aduana	to earn	ganar
to cut	cortar	earth	la tierra
dad	papá	to eat breakfast	desayunar
to dance	bailar	to eat dinner	cenar
dark	oscuro(a)	to eat lunch	comer, almorzar
date	la fecha	economic	económico(a)
daughter	la hija	elegant	elegante
day	el día	embassy	la embajada
to decide	decidir	empty	vacío(a)
to delay	tardar	end	el fin
dentist	el/la dentista	to end	terminar
department store	los almacenes	English	inglés/inglesa

enjoy	**disfrutar de**	(*in a block*)	**el piso**
enough	**bastante,**	flower	**la flor**
	suficiente	food	**la comida**
to enroll	**matricularse**	foot	**el pie**
to enter	**entrar**	on foot	**a pie**
entertaining	**divertido(a)**	football	**el fútbol**
envelope	**el sobre**	for	**para, por**
evening	**la tarde**	for example	**por ejemplo**
event	**el acon-**	fourth	**cuarto(a)**
	tecimiento	free	**libre**
ever	**nunca, jamás**	French	**francés/francesa**
every	**todo/a/os/as**	Friday	**viernes**
excellent	**estupendo(a)**	friend	**el amigo/**
excursion	**la excursión**		**la amiga**
excuse me	**perdón, perdone**	frightened	**asustadol(a)**
to export	**exportar**	from	**de, desde**
eye	**el ojo**	fruit	**la fruta**
face	**la cara**	furniture	**los muebles**
family	**la familia**	garage	**el garaje**
famous	**famoso(a)**	garden	**el jardín**
far	**lejos**	German	**alemán/alemana**
farm	**la granja**	to get off	**bajar de**
fat	**gordo(a)**	to get on	**subir a**
father	**el padre**	to get up	**levantarse**
to feed	**alimentar, dar**	gift	**el regalo**
	de comer	girl	**la chica**
few	**pocos(as)**	to give	**dar**
fiancé	**el novio**	glass	**el vaso**
fiancée	**la novia**	(*material*)	**el cristal**
fifth	**quinto(a)**	glasses	**las gafas**
film	**la película, el**	to go	**ir**
	film	to go away	**irse**
to find	**encontrar**	to go on holiday	**ir de vacaciones**
fine (*noun*)	**la multa**	to go out	**salir**
to finish	**terminar**	to go to bed	**acostarse**
fire	**el fuego**	good	**bueno(a)**
firm	**la empresa**	goodbye	**adiós**
first	**primero(a)**	government	**el gobierno**
fish	**el pescado**	grandfather	**el abuelo**
to fish	**pescar**	grandmother	**la abuela**
flat	**el piso**	grapes	**las uvas**
floor	**el suelo**	green	**verde**

greetings	**los saludos**	hundred	**cien**
group	**el grupo**	hungry	**el hambre**(*f*)
guide	**el/la guía**	to hurt	**doler**
guitar	**la guitarra**	husband	**el marido**
hair	**el pelo**	I	**yo**
hairdresser's	**la peluquería**	ice-cream	**el helado**
hake	**la merluza**	if	**si**
half	**la mitad**	ill	**malo(a),**
ham	**el jamón**		**enfermo(a)**
hand	**la mano**	immediately	**en seguida**
handball	**el balonmano**	important	**importante**
handsome	**guapo**	in	**en**
to happen	**pasar**	in front of	**delante de**
harbour	**el puerto**	in spite of	**a pesar de**
to hate	**odiar**	insurance	**la compañía de**
to have	**tener**	company	**seguros**
to have time	**tener tiempo**	interview	**la entrevista**
to have to	**tener que**	to interview	**entrevistar**
he	**él**	to introduce	**presentar**
head	**la cabeza**	island	**la isla**
health	**la salud**	Italian	**italiano(a)**
heart	**el corazón**	jacket	**la chaqueta**
to heat (up)	**calentar**	jeans	**los vaqueros**
hello!	**¡hola!**	jersey	**el jersey**
to help	**ayudar**	jeweller's shop	**la joyería**
here	**aquí**	job	**el puesto,**
to hire	**alquilar**		**el trabajo**
holidays	**las vacaciones**	joke	**la broma**
home	**la casa**	juice	**el zumo**
homework	**los deberes**	to keep	**guardar**
to hope	**esperar**	key	**la llave**
hospital	**el hospital**	kilo	**el kilo**
hot	**caliente**	to kill	**matar**
hotel	**el hotel**	kiss	**el beso**
hour	**la hora**	kitchen	**la cocina**
house	**la casa**	knee	**la rodilla**
how?	**¿cómo?**	knife	**el cuchillo**
however	**sin embargo**	to know	**conocer** (*a*
how many?	**¿cuántos(as)?**		*place, a*
how much?	**¿cúanto?**		*person*)
hug	**el abrazo**		**saber** (*a fact*)
to hug	**abrazar**	lake	**el lago**

lamp	**la lámpara**	map	**el mapa**
land	**la tierra**	market	**el mercado**
language	**la lengua**	married	**casado(a)**
large	**grande**	to marry	**casarse**
last	**el último/**	maybe	**a lo mejor,**
	la última		**igual, quizás**
late	**tarde**	meal	**la comida**
Latin America	**América Latina**	to meet	**encontrarse**
lawyer	**el, la abogado**	meeting	**la reunión**
to learn	**aprender**	Mexican	**mexicano(a)**
leather	**el cuero**	milk	**la leche**
left	**la izquierda**	mineral water	**el agua**
leg	**la pierna**		**mineral**
lemon	**el limón**	Ministry	**el Ministerio**
less	**menos**	mirror	**el espejo**
letter	**la carta**	Miss	**(la) señorita**
letterbox	**el buzón**	modern	**moderno(a)**
lettuce	**la lechuga**	Monday	**lunes**
life	**la vida**	money	**el dinero**
lift	**el ascensor**	month	**el mes**
light bulb	**la bombilla**	moon	**la luna**
like	**como**	more	**más**
to like	**gustar**	morning	**la mañana**
to listen	**escuchar**	most of all	**sobre todo**
little	**pequeño(a)**	mother	**la madre**
to live	**vivir**	motorway	**la autopista**
lively	**animado(a)**	Mr	**(el) señor**
to look after	**cuidar**	Mrs	**(la) señora**
to look at	**mirar**	museum	**el museo**
to look for	**buscar**	music	**la música**
to look like	**parecer**	must	**deber**
lorry	**el camión**	name	**el nombre**
to love	**amar, querer**	narrow	**estrecho(a)**
luck	**la suerte**	near	**cerca de**
lunch	**el almuerzo,**	nearly	**casi**
	la comida	it is necessary	**hay que**
luxurious	**lujoso(a)**	to need	**necesitar**
magazine	**la revista**	nephew	**el sobrino**
to make	**hacer**	never	**nunca**
man	**el hombre**	new	**nuevo(a)**
to manage to do	**conseguir**	newspaper	**el periódico**
manager	**el director**	niece	**la sobrina**

night	**la noche**	to pay	**pagar**
no	**no**	peach	**el melocotón**
north	**el norte**	pear	**la pera**
North American	**norte-americano(a)**	pen	**el boli, el bolígrafo**
not	**no**	pencil	**el lápiz**
nothing	**nada**	people	**la gente**
number	**el número**	pepper	**el pimiento**
to obtain	**obtener, conseguir**	per cent	**por ciento**
occupation	**la profesión**	perfect	**perfecto(a)**
of	**de**	perhaps	**quizás, a lo mejor**
of course!	**¡claro!**	person	**la persona**
office	**la oficina**	petrol	**la gasolina**
official	**oficial**	petrol station	**la gasolinera**
often	**muchas veces**	photograph	**la foto**
oil	**el aceite**	picture	**el dibujo**
OK	**muy bien, vale**	pig	**el cerdo**
old	**viejo(a)**	plane	**el avión**
olive	**la aceituna**	platform	**la plataforma**
omelette	**la tortilla**	to play	**jugar** (*games*)
on	**en, sobre**		**tocar** (*music*)
once	**una vez**	police force	**la policía**
onion	**la cebolla**	policeman	**el policía**
only	**sólo**	pollution	**la con-taminación**
open	**abierto(a)**		
to open	**abrir**	poor	**pobre**
orange	**la naranja**	postcard	**la postal**
outskirts	**las afueras**	post office	**el correos**
oven	**el horno**	potato	**la patata**
overcoat	**el abrigo**	prawn	**la gamba**
to owe	**deber**	to prepare	**preparar**
owner	**el dueño, la dueña**	at present	**actualmente**
		price	**el precio**
packet	**el paquete**	problem	**el problema**
page	**la página**	puncture	**el pinchazo**
painter	**el pintor, la pintora**	to put	**poner**
		to put on	**ponerse**
painting	**el cuadro**	question	**la pregunta**
parents	**los padres**	quick	**rápido(a)**
to park	**aparcar**	quite	**bastante**
passport	**el pasaporte**	radio	**la radio**

rain	**la lluvia**	to send	**enviar**
to rain	**llover**	sentence	**la frase**
to read	**leer**	serious	**grave**
ready	**listo(a),**	she	**ella**
	preparado(a)	sheet	**la sábana**
receptionist	**el/la**	shellfish	**el marisco**
	recepcionista	shirt	**la camisa**
record	**el disco**	shoe	**el zapato**
record-player	**el tocadiscos**	shop	**la tienda**
red	**rojo(a)**	short	**corto(a)**
relative	**el, la pariente**	to show	**mostrar**
to remain	**quedar**	shower	**la ducha**
to remember	**recordar,**	to sign	**firmar**
	acordarse	signature	**la firma**
to rent	**alquilar**	sister	**la hermana**
to rest	**descansar**	size (*clothes*)	**la talla**
restaurant	**el restaurante**	to ski	**esquiar**
to return	**regresar**	skirt	**la falda**
(*goods*)	**devolver**	small	**pequeño(a)**
rice	**el arroz**	smoke	**el humo**
rich	**rico(a)**	to smoke	**fumar**
right	**la derecha**	to snow	**nevar**
to ring	**llamar a**	socks	**los calcetines**
river	**el río**	soft drink	**el refresco**
road	**la carretera**	son	**el hijo**
room	**la habitación**	song	**la canción**
rug	**la alfombra**	sorry	**lo siento**
to run	**correr**	soup	**la sopa**
salary	**el salario**	south	**el sur**
same	**el mismo, la**	south-east	**el sureste**
	misma	Spain	**España**
sandwich	**el bocadillo**	Spanish	**español/**
sardine	**la sardina**		**española**
Saturday	**sábado**	to speak	**hablar**
sausage	**la salchicha**	to spend	**gastar** (*money*)
to say	**decir**		**pasar** (*time*)
school	**la escuela**	sport	**el deporte**
sea	**el mar**	spring	**la primavera**
season	**la temporada**	squid	**el calamar**
second	**segundo(a)**	stairs	**las escaleras**
to see	**ver**	star	**la estrella**
to sell	**vender**	to start	**empezar**

station	la estación	theatre	el teatro
to stay	quedarse	then	entonces, luego
to steal	robar	there are	hay
still (*adv*)	todavía	there is	hay
stomach	el estómago	therefore	porque
strawberry	la fresa	these	estos/estas
street	la calle	these ones	éstos/éstas
student	el/la estudiante	they	ellos/ellas
to study	estudiar	thief	el ladrón
success	el éxito	thing	la cosa
suit	el traje	to think	pensar
suitcase	la maleta	third	tercero(a)
summer	el verano	thirst	la sed
Sunday	domingo	this	este/esta
surname	el apellido	this one	éste/ésta
sweet	dulce	those	aquellos/
to swim	nadar		aquellas,
swimming-pool	la piscina		esos/esas
to switch off	apagar	those ones	aquéllos/aquél-
to switch on	encender		las, ésos, ésas
table	la mesa	throat	la garganta
to take	tomar	Thursday	jueves
to take a walk	ir de paseo	ticket (cinema)	la entrada para
to take out	sacar		el cine
to talk	hablar	ticket (plane)	el billete de
tall	alto(a)		avión
tape	la cinta	tie	la corbata
taxi	el taxi	timetable	el horario
taxi-driver	el/la taxista	tired	cansado(a)
tea	el té	to	a, hasta
teacher	el profesor/	today	hoy
	la profesora	together	juntos(as)
telephone	el teléfono	toilets	los servicios
telephone box	la cabina	tomato	el tomate
television	la televisión	tomorrow	mañana
to tell	contar	too much	demasiado
temperature	la temperatura	tooth	el diente
tennis	el tenis	toothache	el dolor de
thanks	gracias		muelas
that	aquel/aquella	tourist	el/la turista
that one	aquél/aquélla,	towards	hacia
	ése/ésa	town	la ciudad

to translate	**traducir**	to wear (*clothes*)	**llevar**
to travel	**viajar**	weather	**el tiempo**
travel agency	**la agencia de viajes**	week	**la semana**
		weekend	**el fin de semana**
tree	**el árbol**	welcome!	**¡bienvenido(a)!**
trousers	**los pantalones**	well (*adv*)	**bien**
Tuesday	**martes**	west	**el oeste**
two	**dos**	what?	**¿qué?**
uncle	**el tío**	when?	**¿cuándo?**
underground	**el metro**	where?	**¿dónde?**
to understand	**entender**	where to?	**¿adónde?**
university	**la universidad**	which?	**¿qué?, ¿cuál?**
unmarried	**soltero(a)**	while	**mientras**
unripe	**verde**	white	**blanco(a)**
until	**hasta**	who?	**¿quién?**
up	**arriba**	why?	**¿por qué?**
USA	**los Estados Unidos**	wife	**la mujer**
		wind	**el viento**
to use	**utilizar**	window	**la ventana**
vegetable	**la verdura**	windscreen	**el parabrisas**
very	**muy, mucho**	wine	**el vino**
village	**el pueblo**	with	**con**
to visit	**visitar**	without	**sin**
vocabulary	**el vocabulario**	woman	**la mujer**
to wait	**esperar**	to work	**trabajar**
waiter	**el camarero**	world	**el mundo**
waitress	**la camarera**	wrist	**la muñeca**
to walk	**andar**	to write	**escribir**
wallet	**la cartera**	year	**el año**
to want	**querer**	yellow	**amarillo(a)**
war	**la guerra**	yet	**todavía, aún**
to wash	**lavar**	you (familiar)	**tú,** (*pl*) **vosotros(as)**
watch	**el reloj**		
to watch	**mirar**	you (formal)	**usted,** (*pl*) **ustedes**
water	**el agua** (*f*)		
we	**nosotros(as)**	young	**joven**

Index

The numbers refer to the lesson numbers.